My Sandstone Experience
Copyright © 2014 by Tom Hatfield

Printed in the United States of America

Excerpts reprinted from "Thy Neighbor's Wife" used with permission of Gay Talese.

Excerpts reprinted from "Body Pleasure and the Origins of Violence" used with permission of Dr. James W. Prescott.

Excerpts reprinted from "The Finders' Keeper" used with permission of Kenn Thomas, Steamshovel Press.

Excerpts reprinted from "Scripts People Live" used with permission of Dr. Claude Steiner.

Excerpts reprinted from "What happened on the way to the orgy?" used with permission of Mark Dery.

Excerpts reprinted from "Hot & Cool Sex" used with permission of Dr. Robert Francoeur.

Preface

When Sandstone Ranch was first built in 1935 by one of the original land developers of the supposed playground of the stars, Malibu, it was much more than just his estate – it was his kingdom! It had its own laws, its own army, and its own personal life-style right from the beginning. All you have to do is mention the name to one of the real old-timers of The Malibu, many of whom helped build its stone walls, and you'll see an immediate change in their expression. If they start telling you stories about the place, you'd better get comfortable because it may take a while.

In the late sixties, John and Barbara Williamson came to live there with two other people. They had a history of monogamy, adultery, a nuclear family, the Protestant Work Ethic and divorce. John had been raised on a farm in the South, Barbara the same, but in Missouri. Both of them had succeeded in the business world very well, but found that success unfulfilling. They brought with them theories: a General Systems theory, a Communication theory, Ruth Benedict's Synergy, the theories of Maslow, Chardin, Bertalanffy, and many more. They came to Sandstone to build an environment where those theories, and some of John's own, could be tested.

Even the way they acquired the Ranch was unique. One of the popular rock stars of that period had already put a deposit on the place. But his business manager withdrew the money without the singer's knowledge and took "...the last train to..." That left it open for John and Barbara. There was another, even more popular, rock star who had been told about the place, and planned to visit it on his return from an engagement in London. Unfortunately, he was in no shape to visit anyplace when he returned – he was dead.

So the four of them – John and Barbara and Dave and Oralia moved to Sandstone. The first year they lived there was almost their last. It just happened to be the year the heaviest rainfall in the area for decades. For a while, it looked like the whole place was going to slide right off the edge of the plateau into the deep canyon in front of it. As John tells it, the only real casualty was their Jeep. They watched it slowly sink into a mud hole during one of the heavier downpours.

The four of them, with help from others who had been part of the group in Woodland Hills, like the Bulleros, cleaned up the phenomenal mess the rains left, and got down to the business of creating an environment they would all be happy and secure in. What they created bore little resemblance to what they found when they first arrived at the Ranch. There was a great amount of rebuilding, refurbishing, and adding totally new things to the existing environment. But their creation was an important part of many of the theories they were testing, because they stressed the importance of the environment on the individuals.

Many stories have been written in the past four years, but the description of Sandstone usually boiled down to two things: it was some kind of nudist club, or it was some kind of sex club. Granted, we did go nude – when we felt like it, and we did have consensual sex – when we felt like it, but those two descriptions are so superficial.

Some writers worked with our cooperation and some surreptitiously, but none of them actually lived at Sandstone. They were usually there for a short period of time involving one or two visits, and none of them experienced Sandstone within the context of a Primary Relationship. That is, none of them brought their spouses, legal or otherwise, with them. Most of them chose to experience it alone. To all of us who did live there and did have Primary Relationships, it was painfully obvious after reading some of the stories those writers produced that their experience had been diluted to the point of missing the whole idea of Sandstone.

The ones who came with our blessing and cooperation would possibly make three or four visits for interviewing and attending one or two parties. The ones who came on the sly would probably be there for no more than one party. Either way, the individuals got a very small taste of what we were trying to accomplish. The fact that they came without a Primary Relationship is even more important. That they were alone, without a commitment to anyone else, without any responsibility for another person, diluted the experience far too much.

2

What we were doing could only be understood within the context of a relationship. This was the reason we insisted that our members could only attend the twice-weekly parties as couples. In a way, it's unfortunate that we didn't make the same stipulation for the writers. Their behavior was drastically altered from what it would have been if their mates had been there.

All they could see was nudity and sex. They failed to grasp the simple truth that Sandstone was subjective, experiential. It was different for each individual who came to the Retreat. No one else, of the thousands who visited the Retreat, experienced it the same way I did, and I didn't experience it the same way they did.

Two of the reasons I decided to write this book is that I did live at Sandstone, and I did have a Primary Relationship at Sandstone and a number of Satellites. Some of the stories you will read about what happened while I was in a Primary Relationship, and some while I was single. It shouldn't be difficult for the reader to figure out the difference. My behavior changed, and I am well aware of it.

Gay Talese's book, "Thy Neighbor's Wife," has been re-issued, but with only the addition of a Forward and an Afterword. The book does cover a lot of personal history of the Williamsons and a few others prior to the creation of Sandstone Retreat, but there is very little new in it.

As many as twelve people lived and worked at the Ranch (the numbers and the individuals changed constantly. One of my unanswered questions for John Williamson is what criteria he used to select the residents.), yet only a few of them have ever been described in all the literature written about us. I'm not in his book, and even Marty Zitter isn't mentioned until the second iteration of Sandstone opened.

Gay came to Sandstone as a single male, and fell into the same trap all the other writers did. After giving lengthy biographies of the Williamsons and the Bulleros, he concentrated on the sexual aspect of the Retreat. His book is more about the Sex Business in America instead of just sex in America

Did we achieve our goals? I'm not even sure what those were. John supposedly wrote about them in his "turgid" prose, but I know the Inner Community, those of us living there, were never a synergized group. The Williamsons were gone a lot of the final year, 1972, leaving the rest of us leaderless – even though their leadership was ambiguous at best. I believe their lack of input during the editing phase of the movie was a critical mistake.

Sandstone Retreat closed December 28, 1972, and personally, I'm sorry. I felt a little sad when it closed, but since then, after finding out how little else is available, and listening to so many people anxious to experience it, I'm frustrated. During the five years we were in operation, six to eight thousand people had an opportunity to experience Sandstone, and that just wasn't enough. And many of those who did experience Sandstone didn't maintain the relationship long enough to understand the basis of the philosophy. We used to tell people that we would be very happy to be put out of business because we weren't needed, but that definitely wasn't the reason. Our society is becoming more restrictive and Puritanical every year, so there is still a very big need for a Sandstone environment or something similar; a successful, working model of an Intentional Community where people can come and observe, interact, and compare their own value systems and lifestyles, and hopefully, integrate some of what they experience into their own lives in the Cultural Consensus we call society

Introduction

by
Robert Rimmer

In the spring of 1970, I flew to Kirkridge in the Pocono Mountains of Pennsylvania to attend a week-end symposium on alternative lifestyles that was sponsored by Rustum and Della Roy, authors of the joyous book "Honest Sex." When I finally arrived, late Friday evening, fifty or more of the participants had unpacked and were warming themselves around the huge fieldstone fireplace that unifies the communal dining room of the Kirkridge Retreat. Despite the focus of the week-end, most of us were still somewhat shy with each other - as we slowly discovered who was who and why the other was here.

I had scarcely pinned on my "I'm Bob Rimmer" badge when a sandy haired man in his late thirties greeted me.

"I'm John Williamson. My wife, Barbara, and I flew here from California for one purpose. We wanted to meet you." John was staring at me with the intensity of a biologist examining a new specimen under the microscope. For a moment I

4

had the uneasy sensation I was being hypnotized. His cool blue eyes were unwavering and never strayed from my face as he spoke. Was he measuring my potential for some yet unspoken assignment?

"I hope you won't mind," he was saying, "I'm capitalizing on some of your ideas. Barbara and I aren't like some of the people here. Perhaps we're dreamers too, but we have our feet in reality. I'm a businessman. Here's our story. A new concept in living – Sandstone. Read it tonight and let's talk about it tomorrow." He handed me a notebook with thirty or forty loose-leaf typewritten pages. And then he grinning. "And here's a photograph we brought you from one of your admirers. She's Tom Hatfield's daughter, Brandi. Tom is a member of our Inner Community." The photograph was an eight-by-ten of a lovely fifteen-year-old girl. Naked, she had just stepped out of what was obviously an Olympic-size swimming pool. She was smiling at me with a childish lack of self-consciousness.

Late that night, reading John's notes, I discovered that Sandstone was located in Topanga Canyon, California, on top of one of the mountains in the Malibu chain. It was a large Ranch house, a building with an indoor heated swimming pool, a guesthouse, and several outlying cottages on a total of about fifteen acres of land. Far in the distance, across the moonlike mountains, one could see the Pacific Ocean.

The philosophy of Sandstone is "centered upon non-structured experiential processes which will contribute significantly to the release and actualization of the human potential... Only through the intentional development and expansion of the human potential can humankind ever hope to achieve a supportive society relatively free of alienating, life destructive elements..."

I read on, fascinated. "...Essential to Sandstone is that life attitudes and modes of behavior are acquired and subsequently incorporated to a degree dependent on the intensity of felt emotion during living experiences. These attitudes and modes of behavior tend to be self-perpetuating when they are life negative, and in conflict with life fulfillment and growth they produce varying degrees of painful self and social destruction." Was I understanding what I was reading? I wasn't sure. Visionaries often express themselves turgidly. I kept reading. "It's the main purpose of the Sandstone Foundation to perform a broad, interrelated dual task as guided by the concepts and feedback of experiential change..." This had overtones of Esalan and the human potential movement. But

John had warned me at dinner: "Sandstone takes places like Esalan to their logical conclusion."

With a conclusion as far out as John and Barbara Williamson's, John obviously felt it should be wrapped in soft, floating cumulus clouds. But, gradually, John's notes revealed the reality.

The Inner Community of Sandstone, which was already functioning, would ultimately be composed of an intimate group of people who would live in the Ranch house and in surrounding cottages. The community would be carefully chosen - a cross section of upper-income California businessmen, artists, actors, doctors, lawyers, engineers and people with a creative drive [**Author's Note: Similar to John Galt's Community in** *"Atlas Shrugged"*]. They would continue to work at their particular specialties and contribute a small portion of their income to Sandstone. At least a portion of the week they would live on the grounds forming a tightly knit fully intimate community. Sexual sharing between the members of this inner Community, which would not exceed twenty to twenty-five couples, would be a way of life. But it would be a new kind of sexual sharing and most certainly not the kind of sub rosa behavior that occurred in ordinary adulterous relationships. Members of the Inner Community would not only enjoy the spectacular grounds of Sandstone, the comfortable buildings, the expensive indoor swimming pool, but they also would enjoy sex with other members *openly* - not by retreating to the privacy of the Sandstone rooms, but by copulating together (at least some of the time) in the large ground floor fieldstone-fire-placed living room that ran the fifty foot length of the house and that was paralleled by an equally attractive second-floor room above it.

Presumably after a hard day's work, a Sandstone resident would arrive home, wander into the bar on the ground floor, where other members might be sitting around naked, or partly dressed, and if his (or her) mood or the intimacy of the conversation led him into making love with some other member before dinner, or after dinner, or between drinks - if there was mutual interest - he would be free to snuggle with his temporary mate while his wife (or husband) did likewise. Or if he wasn't in the mood, perhaps he might watch others enjoying themselves, or if he preferred, he could continue talking with his friends. Since John and Barbara were already participating in the full sexual life of the growing Inner Community, they made it clear to new members that the intimacies of Sandstone for the Inner Community would proceed to natural, carefree sex with every other member.

In 1970, according to John, he and Barbara had made love with everyone of the other sex in the Inner Community. As John pointed out to me the next day, they both interviewed prospective members of the Inner Community very carefully, particularly to discover whether they could cope with their sexual jealousies. While the Williamsons were still formulating the philosophy of Sandstone 1969 and 1970, they had yet to discover Martin Zitter, the fast-talking public relations specialist who would become executive vice-president of the Sandstone Retreat and Director of the Sandstone Foundation. Two years later at a symposium of sexual mate swapping held at the Ambassador Hotel in Los Angeles, Martin and John, with the help of Robert Francoeur, author of "Eve's New Rib," had finally crystallized the philosophy of Sandstone into an effective popular statement of the interpersonal sexual relationships at Sandstone. Here is an abstract from Martin Zitter's speech, which introduced the McLuhanesque concepts of cool sex and hot sex for the first time:

"Sexual mate swapping, group sex, and swinging are popular terms for sexual pluralism or social sex. Sexual pluralism is non-reproductive sexual activity with more than two persons present or participating. Although sexual pluralism has long been practiced by many cultures, it has only recently come to light as a researchable phenomenon. The following are a few varieties of sexual pluralism in the U.S. today: *The Secret Affair* - uni or bilateral. Usually characterized by guilt and apprehension within a primary relationship. *Serial Polygamy* - Strings of broken monogamous type marriages. *Mate Swapping* - Usually wife swapping. Two or more couples switch off and retire to private rooms. *Swinging* - Open group sex. Lots of people, lots of orgasms. Strict anonymity generally recognized. *Open-Ended Sensuality* - Pure sensual enjoyment which may even transcend genital sexuality.

Participation in sexual pluralism seems to affect individuals and groups profoundly. Part of the work of the Sandstone Foundation for Community Systems Research is the sponsoring of responsible research into such factors as motivation, involvement, environment, community and personal changes with the hope of developing new, more viable sexual values and emphases. To accomplish this, as a first step Sandstone proposes that there are:

Two Views of "Intimacy" Values in Sexual Pluralism:

COOL SEX	HOT SEX
General and diffused feelings	Genitally focused feelings
Engaging, pleasuring	Orgasm obsessed
Integrated and holistic	Segmented-fragmented
Involved and intimate	Casual and impersonal
Spontaneous	Time and place arrangements
Secure environment	Tenuous environment
Light structure - few games	Structured - mostly games
Group nudity optional	Group nudity discouraged
"Knowing"	Fucking
Equalitarian	Male dominated
Synergistic	Entropic
Optional sexuality	Pressure to perform
Few imperatives	Many imperatives
Few altered (drug) states	Frequent drug usage
Expanded relationships	Escape from monogamy
Sex as medium	Sex as end
"Grokking"*	Preservation of social distance

*"Grok means to understand so thoroughly that the observer becomes a part of the observed—to merge, blend, intermarry, lose identity in group experience. It means almost everything that we mean by religion, philosophy, and science—and it means as little to us (because of our Earthly assumptions) as color means to a blind man."

Robert Heinlein
Stranger in a Strange Land"

In 1970, though John and Barbara hadn't fully formulated this hot and cool sex approach, they were well aware that the Inner Community could not support Sandstone or the necessary full-time maintenance personnel without additional income. Thus, they projected an Outer Community, of which there were already a few members, who would pay annual membership dues of $240 and use the Sandstone facilities largely on weekends. The membership fee would provide money not only for care of the grounds and swimming pool but for a full-time resident club manager. A transient membership of five hundred members, if they all didn't arrive on the same weekends, could easily be handled. The Outer Community would enjoy all of the group privileges of the Inner Community as well as have the use of the Ranch house. Weekdays after seven P.M. and Saturdays and Sundays members would arrive, but only as couples and by appointment. Thus the traffic could be controlled and the human scenery changed as members appeared on different weekends. In the membership flyer, Saturday night was advertised for "celebration and dancing, and a kind of living style where your mind and body and being need no longer be strangers to one another but may unite in human good-will."

The Outer community would not only enjoy the same "open-ended sensuality" as the Inner community but the Inner community might eventually initiate some Outer Community members into the joy of sexual sharing. In a sense, the Outer Community would become a testing ground from which John and Barbara were confident they could recruit additional members for the Inner Community. In addition, as the Inner Community grew in size, it could subdivide into smaller groups and create new Sandstones. As John freely admitted to me, in 1970 the Sandstone philosophy was still evolving.

Several years later when I was with Barbara Williamson and Bob Francoeur on the "Dick Cavett Show" (Bob and Anna Francoeur's new book, in process, titled *Hot and Cool Sex*, expands the Sandstone philosophy), Barbara was still pursuing the idea of a nationwide network of Sandstones. She was apparently unconcerned whether the original Sandstone, which by this time was in financial and legal difficulties, would survive. No matter what happened, the idea of Sandstone was here to stay. Barbara had discovered a very wealthy woman friend who she hoped would underwrite an Eastern Sandstone in the vicinity of Washington D.C., presumably for the enjoyment of the younger and more swinging elective and public officials, and with less emphasis and publicity than Martin Zitter has generated, which possibly contributed to the California Sandstone's downfall.

Incidentally, Barbara Williamson proved the validity of one aspect of Sandstone. If you saw her on the "Dick Cavett Show," or any other television program on which she appeared, or met her in a conventional atmosphere, she gave the impression of a rather dowdyish, not-too-pretty hausfrau. When I saw her naked – in the Sandstone environment – I couldn't believe that this

9

beautifully shaped, sparkling woman, hugging me, happy to see me again, was the same woman I had met at Kirkridge. Barbara proves that women in their thirties or even forties and fifties can be as alluring and sexually attractive as a twenty-year-old Bunny or Pet.

As I read John's original description of Sandstone, I wondered how he had related Sandstone to my writings. The Inner Community had overtones of *The Harrad Experiment*, but it had no formal structure or value conditioning, and the extent of sexual interchange - as many as twenty couples, who might be copulating together - seemed to sow the seeds of Sandstone's ultimate destruction. Intimacy cannot be subdivided infinitely. Then I realized that I had actually outlined parts of the Sandstone philosophy, not as the main focus but as a sharp contrast to the corporate, committed group marriage style that finally evolved in *Proposition 31*. Here's one of the members of Peter Alberti's S.O.S. Group (Save our Spouses) speaking in this novel, which was published in 1968.

There's nothing written down [Catherine said]. You might say our rules and customs have evolved through experience, some of it sad, some of it quite ugly. Take drinking. We've found that liquor and good fucking don't mix very well, and since our prime purpose is to have sexual fun, none of us drinks more than one or two; largely to get rid of our inhibitions, of which there aren't many left. Basically, the females are in command. We make the arrangements. If we have any philosophy, it shakes down to the idea that we want to stay married. With all our various marital faults and disagreements, we feel that divorce is no answer, though some of us have come pretty close to it. We've seen friends go through numerous divorces and remarriages, and still they come apart at the seams. While we don't think sex is all there is to life, we think there's a natural male drive and probably a female one to experience sex, and through it friendship and communication with more than one person of the opposite sex. Monogamy has created an unnecessary and artificial barrier to that need. For example, a few years ago I was becoming rather stodgy, and Jack, my husband, was ready to divorce me. Bed had become a place to sleep or argue. Somehow or other, because of this group, we've learned how to laugh at ourselves, and we've grown psychologically younger, or at least I have.

Having written that, how could I disagree with Sandstone - except in detail? The following morning John Williamson came to the point. "In a few years

Sandstone will be known throughout the world; Sandstone will give many men and women what they really need. A sexual community of friends, free from jealousy. Barbara and I want you to come and live with us and write the story of Sandstone. Eventually, we hope to make a movie, but we feel you are the one person in the United States who can evoke the true meaning of Sandstone for millions of Americans."

As we talked, the indefinable aura of a man obsessed with his mission – a messiah of sex – hung over John. The intensity and hypnotic quality of his self-assurance almost persuaded me. He wondered how I could be certain that my own ideas of sexual varietism, interwoven with deep intimacy, were more feasible than his world of complete sexual self-expression-without-commitment. Wasn't it possible that simple hedonistic relationships – fun and recreation for both the male and the female – were a more valid concept than my own conviction that sexual joining could lead to ultimate communication as well as an alternate consciousness that was far beyond the drug experience? I could finally only shrug. John and I were obviously looking at the same scenery from the tops of different mountains. But I assured him that I wasn't a one-dimensional utopian, and I was intrigued. Certainly the environment of Sandstone was much saner than the artificial sex-tease atmosphere of a Playboy club. What would the United States be like if one day Holiday Inns were transformed into Sandstones?

A man with a vision has no difficulty in attracting followers. Before the Kirkridge weekend was over John discovered a young psychologist, Stephen Beltz, who was overwhelmed with John Williamson's dream of happy sexual anarchy. Though it took some doing (how he managed to convince his wife, who appeared to be quite middle class and seemed to be one-male oriented, is Stephen's as yet unpublished story), six months later he moved to Sandstone and was appointed research director. His dream of a sexual Land of Oz not only coincided with John and Barbara's, but John had discovered a skilled promotion man. In January of 1971 an elaborate forty-page, spiral-bound prospectus appeared, proposing a five-year funding program for Sandstone, which had now been named The Sandstone Foundation for Community Systems Research, Inc.

The New Sandstone approach, described in glowing term by disciple Stephen with projections, charts, graphs, and explanations, completely disassociated itself from "Growth Centers" and "the human potential movement" by relating Sandstone to normal establishment goals, and by emphasizing that Sandstone "has a transcendental purpose of working to improve society by developing new

11

group lifestyles and communities." The prospectus pointed out that growth centers preach depth relationships among people, but block open sexuality. Sandstone encouraged total relationships on a continuing basis - including open, honest sexuality among consenting adults.

With great seriousness the prospectus sought a funding of $3 million. In deference perhaps to more sober philanthropists the personal sexual aspects of Sandstone were played down and the emphasis was placed on sexual research, model building (a study of the group organism), measurement development techniques, individual change techniques, natural and intentional groups, community functioning, and so forth, and so on. In addition, Stephen included a research proposal for the study of communes and intentional communities.

As Stephen had stated in the prospectus, the reasons for taking his wife and five children to Sandstone were complex, but basically were oriented around what he was convinced would eventually be a steppingstone to the New Society. Were Stephen's daydreams punctured by the actual facts of day-to-day existence at Sandstone? Whatever happened (no doubt an inability to come to terms with a family life in the environment of open sexuality), Stephen disappeared.

Addendum

Sometimes when I can't write, I do searches on the Web for people who were part of Sandstone back in the 70s. Stephen Beltz has always interested me, or more specifically, the forty-page Prospectus we created for the Sandstone Foundation that included a budget of three million dollars. I've asked John about it, and he doesn't have it, although he reminded me that I helped write it. That means the Prospectus was probably the presentation we made to IBM.

I only met Stephen once. I was living in Trancas Canyon with Pam. and the kids when Stephen and his family arrived at the Ranch. I went up to the Ranch to borrow something, and briefly met Stephen and his wife, Judith. I saw their kids walking down toward the pool. What Rimmer didn't mention is that Stephen and his family arrived at the Ranch in a big yellow school bus (shades of Ken Kesey and the Pranksters!).

So I recently did a Yahoo! Search on his name hoping that he might still have a copy of the Prospectus. I believe I'd done it before and came up with nothing. This time I hit pay dirt, because the synopsis mentioned his wife, Judith, so I knew it was the right Stephen Beltz.

The search led me to a web site called [CTRL], and an interview titled, "The Finder's Keeper, Marion Pettie," by Kenn Thomas, Steamshovel Press – which specializes in publishing material about conspiracies – like the Kennedy assassination, or 9/11. At first, I didn't know what I was looking at. How did this article relate to Stephen Beltz?

The article begins by trying to define The Finders. Depending on who you believe, a 1994 reference work- on utopian communities refers to the Finders as "a rather spontaneous non-organization ... Their overall approach to life is to make it into a game--a challenging and educational process where the rules change from week to week, day to day, sometimes even by the hour."

Or you can believe investigator Ted Gunderson's handwritten description, attached to Treasury Department memoranda on the Finders that Ted Gunderson circulates in an info-packet about the group: "the Finders are a CIA front established in the 1960s. It has TOP CLEARANCE and PROTECTION in its ASSIGNED task of kidnapping and torture-programming young children throughout the US. Members are specially trained GOVERNMENT KIDNAPPERS known to be sexual degenerates who involve children in Satanic sex orgies and bloody rituals as well as murders of other children and slaughter of animals."

During a raid on Finders properties in Washington D.C. "...men seized evidence they said may have been indicative of an organized ring of pedophilic child kidnappers who made animal sacrifices to Satan." Supposedly, documents found at the Finders property "revealed detailed instructions for obtaining children for unspecified purposes. The instructions included the impregnation of female members of the community known as the Finders, purchasing children, trading, and kidnapping." One memo claimed that the "CIA made one contact and admitted to owning the Finders organization as a front for a domestic computer training operation, but that it had gone bad." The operation was called Future Enter Pages.

Wow! That's a little heavy. Please don't tell me Stephen and Judith were mixed up with those people.

I'm not going to repeat the interview with Mr. Pettie, supposedly the leader of the Finders. He denies such an organization ever existed, although the article states that there were about 40 people involved in the Finders. I do have to quote from the article to show the convoluted path from Mr. Pettie to the Beltz family.

13

"In 1971 Pettie infiltrated the 'human potential' movement, setting up Ken Kesey (Living Love) as a prominent guru and working through Dr. Stephen Beltz (related to Judith Beltz) a behavior modification specialist more recently deployed to the Institute of Cultural Affairs and the Meta Network cult." (1971 was shortly after the Beltz family left Sandstone.)

Toward the end of the article, the Beltz name surfaces again; "Pettie's activities took a different turn in 1979 when he recruited John J. Cox, founder of General Scientific (a computer firm specializing in classified defense, contracts). Cox... recruited Susan Gabriel and Judith Beltz as couriers." What Susan and Judith carried, and from where to where, is not mentioned, but it would appear that the Beltz relationship with those people lasted a few years.

Coincidentally, my uncle was in the OSS. I saw him once when I was very young. When I saw my first James Bond movie, I thought of him – he looked just like my uncle. His son, Bill Briggle, became a big man in the Department of the Interior, working in the National Parks System.

I did numerous additional searches on the Finders. There is no lack of documentation on the activities listed above, the CIA connection, or that Marion Pettie was the leader. Even though there is a nebulous third-party connection between Stephen and Judith and Marion Pettie, and the Finders did have a reputation as a Utopian Community, I hope they were not connected to the Finders in any way. Their names did not show up in any additional documents I found. My search added a few more pieces to the puzzle, but it's still missing the whole picture. Back to Rimmer's Introduction;

I met Tom Hatfield for the first time when I was invited to speak at a weekend sponsored by The Happy Company, an association of several hundred people living in group marriages and alternate lifestyles. The locale for the weekend was Sandstone.

In between speeches in the evening, sitting on the living room floor with all the rest of the naked lovers, Tom told me about himself and many of the fascinating stories you'll read in this book. He hoped that one day he would write a book about Sandstone. Was there any more logical candidate? One of the roles he had assumed as a member of the Inner community was that of club manager and he was therefore in close touch with many of the Outer Community. Only John and Barbara knew more about Sandstone than he did. But Tom was discouraged. Gay Talese, the best-selling author of *The Kingdom and the Power* and *Honor Thy Father* was living at Sandstone. Tom didn't like Gay. I think the reason was he didn't feel that Gay was sincere in his interest in Sandstone. But, because of his fame, Gay Talese naturally became John Williamson's choice to write *the* book about Sandstone.

I met Gay the next day. Both of us were strolling, happily naked, around the grounds, enjoying the austere scenery of the Malibu mountains stretched out below us, as well as the equally intriguing movement of *humans being naked together*. Gay was bubbling with enthusiasm. Sandstone was a sexual nirvana. I asked him if he was gathering information for a book. Gay was noncommittal. He admitted he was investigating "the sex industry" (his terminology) in America. If he finally decided to go ahead, Sandstone might be a chapter. I, myself, might be a chapter. But Gay Talese wasn't too sure of me. Unless I was a practitioner, in addition to being a prophet, I might have nothing to add.

It was my turn to be noncommittal. "I'm not a proselytizer," I told him, "nor am I writing my autobiography, yet!"

Later on a radio show with Gay and Marty Zitter, who had become a rather belligerent publicist for Sandstone, refusing to accept the validity of any life-style other than the Mecca in Topanga, I couldn't resist probing the much more taciturn Talese. Since he was openly confessing that being at Sandstone was like being a kid in a candy store, I was curious about the underlying reason for his obsession with the Sandstone philosophy. Was it because at thirty-nine or forty years of age, like most American males, his dreams of sexual varietism had never been fulfilled? He had been brought up in a strict Roman Catholic family and he had survived many years of a faithful marriage. I wondered if Gay was living out his sexual fantasies in an environment that extolled the Frederick S. Perls philosophy of "Do your own thing." Amazingly, Gay Talese's wife, a "private person" to use his own words, was safely at home in New York City, aware of where he was and apparently unconcerned. Despite Gay's insistence in *Oui* Magazine ("If I go to Sandstone, I get involved in Sandstone. I don't feel guilty about it, because my marriage is not one that prompts that reaction in either myself or my wife"), the question remains: Can an outsider living a few months in Sandstone, even as a participating observer **[Without his mate!]**, write about it with the same kind of involvement as a man whose basic life-style *is* Sandstone?

And that's the difference between Tom Hatfield and Gay Talese. We all have different viewpoints on Sandstone, but unless John and Barbara Williamson

15

finally write their autobiography, Tom is the only other person I know who could reveal not only Sandstone as it was, but the kind of personal necessity that made Sandstone a kind of salvation for Tom.

Gay Talese, who may have once considered writing the story of Sandstone, is probably in fundamental agreement with me about sex. I recently wrote an article - which I delight in using as a subject for speeches - titled "Being in Bed Naked with You Is the Most Important Thing in My Life." In the Oui Magazine article, Gay Talese made a parallel statement. "Sex is so important; it is probably the most important thing. What is more important? It is the one great joy of all times - maybe the ultimate, timeless universal joy, or what could be joy."

Tom Hatfield's book is in the same vein. In my opinion, it's an important sociological document, not because I believe in the Sandstone approach to sex but because Sandstone represents one current that may soon vanish in the cold water of censorship. We continue to live in a world where leaders believe they have the right (whether a large minority approve or not) to legislate our morality.

Just as I believe there should be Harrad style and Premar style undergraduate experiences, and that Proposition 31 should be a legalized marriage style, so there should be Sandstones. It is my belief that we must learn how to be naked with each other both quantitatively and qualitatively - and the nakedness of self-disclosure and defenselessness is the sine qua non of great sex. One thing is certain. As you read this book, you can discover the parameters of your own morality. Simply ask yourself, could I go to Sandstone and leave my guilt feelings and needs for extended intimacy with one person at home? Is sex recreation, or is it communication? Could Sandstone have eventually found a way to merge the hot and cool aspects of sex into a viable life-style? Or – let us hope not – is the deification of work and the accumulation of synthetic man-made junk more important than sex and loving?

First Visit to Sandstone

In the early Spring of 1967, Bob Chapman and I decided to publish a Magazine called *Beach*. It would explore the Beach lifestyle and the people who lived there. I was doing research for a story on nudism, or more specifically, nudism at the beach, and I was having a little trouble finding information on the subject. So I went to what I considered a pretty good reference source, the *Los Angeles Free Press*. There was a small, one-line ad in the classifieds that said, "Nudists call 213-XXX-XXXX." I called, a man answered and told me to come to an office on Westwood Blvd. for an interview.

The owner of a motel had rented out the second story rooms as offices, and the last one had a rustic piece of stone on the front door with "Sandstone" hand-lettered on it. As I started up the steps, I felt slightly nervous. The whole thing was a little weird. I'd been in touch with another local organization that practiced nudity, Elysium, and had mentioned Sandstone to them. They were very vague about it, but more from ignorance than anything else. They'd heard about it, but that was all.

The front office was nicely appointed with a beautiful desk, a filing cabinet and a couple of black modern leather chairs. There was no one sitting at the desk, but I heard a voice in the other room, so I walked over to the door and looked in. A nice-looking man in his thirties was sitting at the desk talking on the phone. He seemed to be well-built from the waist up, with a nice face and lots of black curly hair that didn't need combing to look good. When he saw me, he smiled broadly and motioned me to the chair that was watching his animated gestures as he talked. His voice was soft and there was a definite accent.

When he hung up the phone, he stood and introduced himself. "Hi. I'm Albert. What can I do for you?" He turned out to be a little shorter than me, maybe five-ten.

I told him what I was looking for, and how I'd come to call their organization.

"Groovy!"

I discovered later that it was his favorite word. We talked for about an hour, but all I found out for sure was that his accent was Swiss, and that Sandstone was a private club for people who wanted to "express themselves." The sensual pictures on the walls of beautiful people in the nude gave me a good idea of what the expression meant. My excitement grew by leaps and bounds. He seemed very enthusiastic about Sandstone, and also seemed positive that I should visit it. By now my curiosity was at a level where all I could do was agree with him. He gave me a map that showed the location and a couple of different ways of getting there. Some rules were printed at the bottom; The first thing that caught my eye was, "PRIVATE – BY INVITATION ONLY."

The first time I tried to visit Sandstone was a clear, warm Saturday afternoon. For some reason I felt it would be best if I took a friend along, whether for comfort or protection, I'm not sure, and the two of us set off.

We followed the Pacific Coast Highway past the beaches to Topanga Canyon Blvd. we found our way up the narrow, twisting canyon road that leads to the small village of Topanga, which has become an enclave of retreat from the madness of neighboring Los Angeles. Just before we reached the village, I took the indicated turnoff, and started up a steep, winding road that was supposed to take us to the Ranch. Unfortunately, we never made it – the steep climb was too much for the car. It over-heated and blew a radiator hose. We had to coast all the way back down to the service station in the village. Naturally, we were both disappointed. Our fantasies were running rampant.

A few days later I tried again. This time I made sure the car was in good shape, and I went alone. I had no trouble conquering the mountain that had defeated me before, and I found the stone pillars that guarded the entrance to Sandstone.

The view was Magnificent! All the south coast from Santa Monica to the Palos Verdes Peninsula was visible with Catalina island peeking through a low lying fog bank offshore. The last half mile was on a dirt road that could have stood some work, but I was too excited to care. I reached the bottom of a short hill and I was there.

My first impression of Sandstone was astonishment!

There, sitting at the top of a deep, rugged canyon, on a series of natural plateaus was a very beautiful estate surrounded on all sides by enormous Eucalyptus trees. One of the first things that struck me as I walked

down the driveway toward the main house was the cleanliness of the whole place. The driveways were swept clean of leaves, the lawns were well-trimmed, and the flowers that were just beginning to bloom were very neat with an absence of weeds. Somebody spent a lot of time keeping all of this looking so good. By the time I reached the front door, I had a million questions.

Tentatively, I knocked on the big front door, and heard a laughing voice say, "Come in."

When I opened the door, there stood an absolutely beautiful, dark-skinned woman – totally nude! That stopped me cold for a minute, and we just looked at each other. She must have been the laughing voice I heard, because there was still a smile on her face as she finally spoke, "Can I help you?"

Never mind all the obvious, smart-ass replies I could have made. All I said was, "I'm looking for John or Barbara Williamson."

Her head turned to the right, and she indicated two people sitting on the couch. "That's them.

"Thank you." She smiled and disappeared around the corner.

As I walked toward the couch, I had the feeling I should be walking on tip-toe, as if I were in a very large cathedral. The room was about twenty feet wide and sixty feet long. It was broken in the center by a group of three couches around a large, low, glass-topped coffee table that held a few Magazines and ash trays. There were two smaller tables at the corners of the couches, and they held two very tall lamps. The thick, shag carpeting was a beautiful rich gold, and the couches were just a shade darker. The tables were made of a very dark wood, and the combination made the room one of the warmest, richest settings I'd ever been in. The couches faced a large, brick fireplace that went from the floor to the ceiling with its enormous beams, and reigned over the whole room.

I introduced myself to two more nude people. John was my age, about 36, a little shorter and very well built. As we shook hands, a small spark jumped across our fingertips and I flinched. John laughed, and told me it didn't happen unless you were wearing shoes. Intense, with soft blue eyes, he looked directly at me as

19

he spoke. I found it necessary to move a little closer to him because of his soft voice. Some people said this was a mechanism he used to hold your attention, but it seemed perfectly natural to me. After spending so much time in the noise-riddled city, it was nice to be in an environment where a person could be heard without shouting.

Barbara looked like a Midwestern school teacher – until you looked at her body. It was near perfect! She must have been in her mid-thirties, but she took such great care of herself that her body looked twenty. One writer has referred to her "…sixteen year-old boobs." Her breasts were much too beautiful to be labeled with that word.

John asked me what type of research I was doing, and I tried to explain that I was attempting to start a new Magazine concerned with different aspects of living at the beach. I told him that it was my observation that "beach people" were a little different from other geographical groups, and I was interested in examining that difference. One thing I noticed was a freer acceptance of their bodies, expressed in their clothing or lack of it, and the growing interest in nude beaches. I wanted to find out more about that part of the lifestyle.

I told John that I'd heard of the Free beach up in Northern California, and a couple of clandestine secluded beaches locally, but I was interested in any organized movement by nudist groups toward achieving the legal status of Clothing Optional beaches. John and Barbara seemed very interested in what I was saying, and didn't interrupt with any questions or let anything else in the room detract from their interest, but I was slightly distracted by a few things. Like the phone. The ringing didn't bother me, but whenever it rang, the dark-skinned beauty would come bouncing into the room to answer it. Her small, up-turned breasts would dance, and her very nice, round ass would quiver a little as she walked past us.

Then John started telling me about "The Sandstone Foundation for Community Systems Research." He told me of the long-range goal of a teleocratic, synergistic large-scale community (words I honestly didn't understand), and about the five of them who lived at Sandstone presently; John and Barbara, Dave and Oralia (the dark-skinned beauty), and Albert, whose main function was to run Sandstone Retreat as the financial base of their community.

20

He told me how the Retreat operated as a private club whose members paid an annual fee that entitled them to use the luxurious environment any day except Monday. He explained that the club had parties every weekend, which was the time most members took  advantage of the facilities. These parties featured almost total freedom as far as behavior was concerned, and included optional nudity and open sexuality. Nudity I understood, but the "open sexuality" was another mystery to me. The talk was mostly about their community in relationship to many of the other experiments being tried around the country. We talked for the need for more communication between all of the different groups that were attempting to find an "alternate lifestyle." That's where I came in; they also wanted to publish a Magazine, and wanted my help on that and other graphics projects.

"Would you like a tour of the place, Tom?" John caught me a little off-guard with that, I was still visualizing some of the fantastic possibilities the place offered for graphics.

"Sure," I replied, "Where do we start?"

"Let's go this way." He led me from the living room, past an enormous sketch of David's head, into the dining room. A four-foot high wood planter filled with beautiful greenery divided it from the living room.

The dining room contained an eight-foot, glass-topped wooden table surrounded by eight high-backed chairs, and a huge breakfront. The same carpeting that was in the living room extended all the way through the dining room.

We continued on to a small, by comparison, kitchen that had the normal appliances and dark wood cabinets. Then we made two sharp right turns that put us at the top of a steep, narrow staircase. John flipped a light switch that revealed deep-red carpeting covering the stairs, but gave no hint of where they led. I couldn't see anything at the bottom.

When we reached the bottom, John flipped another light switch and a large room glowed, probably twenty by eighty feet, and I finally began to understand what he meant by open sexuality.

"I guess you could call this our Party Room, Tom. It's where most of the activity takes place." There were six mattresses spaced around the room covered with brightly colored sheets. That was all, except for two small tables. The room was dominated by the fantastic red carpeting that almost dazzled you. Plus the fact that the lighting was also red, which gave everything in the room a glow – including us.

There was a small bar at the far end of the room with three stools in front of it and a large mirror behind it. The walls had three-dimensional artwork hanging on them that I couldn't decipher. I felt better when John told me, "They make more sense if you're stoned when you look at them."

We walked around the bar and through two doorways, no doors, with a small bathroom between them, and into another room that had a stall shower, a vanity with a mirror, and wall-to-wall mattresses.

"People call this the Ball Room."

I had a million questions going through my mind, but felt kind of foolish asking them. I found out later that this was a mistake. John rarely offered any information about something, but he was usually willing to answer questions. I was trying to act nonchalant about the whole thing, but I doubt if I fooled him.

We re-traced our way back to the bar, then John pulled back some drapes exposing a sliding glass door. "Let's go this way." He led me out into a driveway, and I got an even bigger electric shock when I touched the door frame. John saw me wince. "Going to have to do something about getting rid of those shoes, Tom."

The driveway led down past a terraced lawn to a parking lot. We stood on the edge of it for a minute, and the view was awesome. The canyon dropped off abruptly into a deep gorge that ran all the way to the ocean, and held some rugged rock formations. The hillsides were green, and Spring flowers were beginning to bloom.

We turned and walked up the driveway beside the house under some enormous eucalyptus trees. Neither of us spoke for a few minutes, then John broke the silence. "Let me show you the swimming pool."

"Great." I was still dazed by all this. There was too much to assimilate at one time.

22

We continued past the house and the courtyard in front of it to a large building that I had assumed was another house when I'd seen it earlier. It, too, was large, probably eighty by fifty. We walked up the stone steps to a pair of sliding glass doors which John opened.

The first thing I noticed was a definite increase in the air temperature, even though it was a warm, sunny day outside. Cedar beams ran the width of the building, holding up the ceiling of fiberglass panels that allowed the sunlight to filter through.

John told me, "We keep the water temperature about 92 degrees. Very relaxing." I noticed a small room at the back of the pool and asked about it.

"That's a bathroom with a shower," John said as we left the pool building. "There are some smaller houses around here where the other members of the family live, and that's about it. Actually, the whole place is fifteen acres, but we're only using this part of it right now."

John talked some more about their proposed Magazine as we walked back to the main house and joined Barbara in the living room. He asked me about my home life, and I told him about Pam. and the kids and what an open family we had; how the kids and I went nude around the house, and how we were always ready to talk about sex with the kids if they had any questions. I thought I should let him know that this wasn't too different from what I was into. When I finished, he said, "That sounds good, Tom. By the way, have the kids ever seen you and Pam. make love?"

"Uh...no, not really..." Hell, I didn't even see us make love! She always insisted I turn the lights out. (Since Sandstone, if a woman questions the lights, I whisper softly in her ear, "I like to see what I'm eating") I felt a little embarrassed getting put in my place that way. These people took 'liberal' to extremes I could barely imagine. I had a very strong feeling that my life was going to go through some big changes, and that I'd finally found what I'd been looking for. I wasn't even sure what it was, but

I knew I'd found it.

Between the warm environment we were in, and this quiet man's convincing words, beautiful Barbara's lovely breasts, and that outrageously exquisite dark-skinned woman named Oralia, I really had no choice. Their Magazine sounded like a much better idea than mine, so I immediately accepted their offer to become part of the Sandstone Foundation for Community Systems Research!

A few days later, John and Barbara made one of their rare trips down the mountain to our house. We had moved out of the condo complex, and now lived in a lovely, older two-story house on top of a hill in Hermosa beach. It was the first time my family had met them, and all of us were a little uncomfortable by the occasion. All in all, though, it went well. I was a little surprised to see them in clothes, although the thought of them making the trip nude was slightly ridiculous. It didn't take long for them to make everyone, except Pam., feel very comfortable.

We discussed plans for the proposed Magazine a little, and a few other things they were considering. It was agreed that I'd be employed as the Managing Editor of the Magazine, and would receive ten percent of net profit from it, plus a salary to be determined at a later date. Since there was nothing in their treasury to pay me with presently, there was no sense in setting a figure. I would also be given complete access to all of the facilities at Sandstone. That last clause was the real clincher. Just to be able to go back to that Magic place and see more of the people would have been enough inducement for me to join their organization. They suggested I contact Ed Lange at Elysium Fields in Topanga for more information on nude beaches. So I did.

Elysium Fields was another C.O. resort. I met Ed Lange, a well-known photographer – tall, fit, full white beard, he could have been type-cast to play God, wearing a long Kaftan. I explained what information I was looking for and told him a little about the proposed Magazine. Elysium also published a Magazine, Ankh, but it was not available on your local newsstand – by subscription only. Ed was extremely generous with information about nude beaches, and even gave me a half-dozen photos I could use in exchange for a quarter-page advertisement. That opened up a whole new can of worms; advertising rates. So based on Ed's input and rate cards I received from two other Magazines, I put together a rate card for Beach. Ed also gave me a free-pass card for Elysium so I could bring my family for a visit – I used that card later.

We had two issues almost ready to go to press when we got smacked upside the head by Reality – in the form of distribution. The first question we were asked by a potential distributor was, "Why should I distribute your Magazine?" He informed us what his cut of the sale price would be, then asked if we had any preference as to where the Magazine would be placed on the newsstand racks. Higher up and more visible locations did increase his cut. When he mentioned up-front money, we finally realized we didn't have the initial capital to pay printers and distributors. So much for publishing a new Magazine!

Before Sandstone

At the time I made my initial contact with Sandstone, I was living with a woman and her four children. We weren't legally married, but the relationship had lasted five years and we both considered ourselves married. It was a totally monogamous relationship. After two previous relationships that hadn't been exactly monogamous. I decided to try and make this one really work the way I'd been told the way a relationship was supposed to work.

My first marriage had been to a girl of 17 when I was 21. It lasted two short years and I had "played around" during that time.. Ours was an example of a neurotic marriage. She refused to surrender her virginity until she was legally married, so I married her. We really had nothing in common. I was hustling pool in bars and meeting a lot of women, racing power boats and skin-diving, and she hated my boat and going underwater. She was on the phone with her high-school friends.

So the only basis for our relationship was a physical one, and that just wasn't enough – especially since her refusal to have oral-genital relations made even the physical bond unsatisfactory to me.

I awoke one morning to find her standing in the doorway looking at me. That was okay, but I didn't see my wife. Somehow, I thought I was seeing a girl I was having an affair with, and couldn't figure out what she was doing there.

"Sweetheart!" (Fortunately, I didn't use names) "What are you doing here?"

My wife looked a little perplexed when she answered, "I just wanted to let you know breakfast is ready."

"Ummm, come here baby." She came over and sat on the bed next to me. I put my arms around her and held her very close for a minute before it hit me. Holy shit! This isn't Betty! It's my wife! Well, that scared me. It also got me thinking about the relationship.

Later that same day I drove our new Plymouth to a bar to meet a friend. We were close friends for different reasons, and one was because we shared the same girlfriend. We spent the afternoon shooting pool and drinking beer and eating pickled ham-hocks. Just to make the games more interesting, we'd make various wagers on the games. Neither of us had a lot of money, so the bets would be more esoteric; like nights of the week we'd spend with our mutual girlfriend. We'd been playing for a couple hours before we had trouble finding things to bet.

My friend asked, "You driving that flashy new car today?"

"Yeah. Why?"

"Well, you've always had your eye on my motorcycle, and I thought I might like to drive a new car for a while, so let's play for pink slips."

I had to think about that for a minute. There was no doubt that my car was worth a lot more than his Harley K model. The bike had been through it. It even had steel tubes for rear shocks. But I knew I was a better shooter than he was and not quite so drunk. So his only chance of winning was sheer luck, but he did have it once in a while. Actually, I don't think either of us had the real pink lips in our possession. I know mine was at some bank that was financing the car, and the motorcycle could be stolen.

He's already racked the balls, so I broke and we played the game. I won.

"Well, I guess you win the bike. Will you let me use it once in a while until I can afford to buy a car?"

"Sure, buddy." I tend to get Magnanimous when I drink too much. "Right now, I'm going to pick up my wife – she's working today. I'll show her the bike, and bring it back. See you later."

I went out and got on the bike. After almost breaking my leg trying to kick-start it, I took off and arrived in the parking lot at my wife's business. I spun a few doughnuts waiting for her. Finally I saw her coming out of the building, and after I yelled a few times, she recognized me and began walking toward the bike.

"What the hell is that thing?"

"Come on, you know what it is."

"Where's my new car?"

"Oh, it's up at the bar. Climb on and we'll go get it."

"You really expect me to get on that thing?" She seemed to be upset. Maybe I drank a little too much. "I'm not moving from this spot until you get my new car!"

Without saying a word, I started the bike and rode away. When I got back in the car, she was standing in the same spot. We got in the car and headed home.

After we left the parking lot, she said, "We're not doing too good, Tom."

"Yeah, I know." I started sobering up fast.

"I think we should break up for a while. Maybe it would help."

"Yeah, maybe it would."

So by mutual agreement, she moved back in with her parents. Less than a week later, I came home from work to find a moving van parked in front of our apartment, and a U.S. Marshall watching two guys emptying the apartment. I was served with the divorce papers by the Marshall when I asked what the hell was going on.

My second marriage was five years later. I was racing sports cars instead of boats, and she was working for the Women's Sports Car Club at the races. I remember the Saturday night dinner for everyone involved and she was sitting across the table. My pit man and me secretly flipped a coin to see which of us would score with her. She was flirting with both of us. I won.

I didn't just score, I hit a home run! She told me two weeks later she was pregnant. Well, the only gentlemanly thing to do was marry her. That's what I was told when I was growing up. She suggested an abortion, but I said no. she came on so innocent and scared I just had to do the right thing.

Then a few weeks before the ceremony (money spent on invitations, the church and reception hall), She decide to tearfully admit all. She was far from innocent! She'd had sex with about ten other race car drivers, lived with a guy for a little while, had an affair with a married man, and had a previous abortion. After telling me this, she turned to me and said, "I don't suppose you want to marry me now."

But I lived up to those finer principles my parents had instilled and replied, "Of course I'll still marry you."

The marriage produced two beautiful boys and lasted a little over five years. I went into the marriage vowing to that I would try and make it work, but like other vows I'd made, didn't last long. A few months after the wedding I took a temporary contract job in San Diego. It kept getting extended. The situation was definitely not conducive to maintaining a monogamous relationship based on my value system, and I didn't.

It was really confusing. I'd go into a relationship planning to be faithful, but it just didn't work. I'd meet a pretty girl who turned me on, and I'd want to do something about it. There weren't many one-night-stands. They were involved relationships that required a lot of lying, planning, and deceit on my part. That bothered me. I know the road to hell is paved with good intentions, I bought a few miles of it during that time.

Toward the end of the second marriage my son told his mom he'd seen me kissing her friend in the kitchen the day before. I hadn't been, didn't even like her fiend that much, she and I both told my wife it didn't happen, but because of my past affairs, I had trouble convincing her.

Finally, I promised my wife that if I was planning to have an affair with any woman, I'd break up the marriage. I met the woman and divorced my wife.

Pamela and I were both working for the same publications job shop. She was in the typing department and I was in the art department. We both worked the night shift, and because of the nature of our work, we spent a lot of time together in a professional relationship before it ever became personal. I'd find excuses to go in the typing department.

Finally, we started having lunch together, then going out for a beer after work. I let the relationship develop slowly, because she seemed reluctant to get too involved. She told me she'd heard about me from other girls and she didn't want to be one of my "conquests."

At one point, my boss took me out to lunch and told me I'd have to stop seeing her away from the office or he'd have to take more drastic steps. I told him to get fucked and he took me seriously – called my wife to see if she'd go out with him

The night he fired me, I decided to move in with Pamela and her four children, 3 girls and a boy, 10, 8, 6, and 4. Three different fathers. I found a new job within a week.

When my newly adopted family started living together, it was in a new house that Pamela's mom had put a down-payment on. It wasn't really a bad house considering where they had been living in a subsidized apartment complex, but it just one of 300 homes that made up a condominium complex in a town called Norwalk, CA.

I had spent almost my entire life within walking distance of the Pacific Ocean and my lifestyle reflected that. My baby-sitters had introduced me to it when I was four. Beach people are more liberal than Flatlanders. Their first impression of me was that that I was a radical liberal. The only thing really radical about me was a rather scraggly beard and my outlook on young people.

It didn't take us long to discover that we had practically nothing in common with our new neighbors and no interest in the social life of the community – which consisted of square-dancing and card playing in the community center. Most of our time was spent working very long hours on the Swing shift and laying beside the community swimming pool during the day. We moved there over the Easter week-end, so we had the mixed blessing of very warm weather. The blessing was mixed because we could get a nice tan, but Norwalk is located in the middle of the dairy industry. We had to put up with the odor and the flies.

Her oldest daughter is the one who got me involved with the young people living in and around the complex. She came in the door one afternoon looking very upset and slammed the door behind her.

"It's not fair! It's just not fair!"

I had a feeling I was being baited, but I jumped in anyway. "What's not fair?"

"Oh, the way they treat the guys," she replied, flopping down on the couch.

"What are you talking about? Or would you rather not talk about it?" I wasn't sure of my status with the kids, so I always stepped lightly in these areas.

"It's the damn Board of Governors. They're the ones causing all the trouble." Either she didn't hear my second question or she was giving me permission to ask more questions.

I'd better point out that the social activity in the complex was controlled by a Board of Governors that was elected annually by the residents. There was also an overseer paid by the developer to watch out for his interests. It was supposed to be their form of democracy. This wasn't the first time I'd heard about rulings of the Board that many of the young people didn't agree with. Recently, they had decided to close the swimming pool certain days of the week - during one of the famous hot spells. "So what did they do this time?" I asked.

"It's just not fair, Tom." She stood up and started pacing the floor as she talked. "They're going to let the Girl's Teen Club (sneer) have dances in the town hall, but they won't let the boys do the same."

"Honey, I don't understand. What difference does it make who throws the dances? You all get to go. Right?"

"Well, yeah. But it makes a big difference because if the girls have the dance,

29

we have to wear dresses and the guys have to wear coats and ties. Besides, the guys can get the best music. They know all the good bands around here."

"What's wrong with wearing a dress? You look damn good in that Mandarin mini-dress I got you." I took her to the annual Christmas party at Laufer Publishing where I worked on the teen Magazines, Tiger Beat and Fave. She was slightly popular!

"Ha! Thanks, I love it, but it's really short and the slits up the side to my waist are just too sexy for this place! You can see my underwear – if I wear any." She smiled.

"Well, why can't the guys throw their own dance? They live here too." That's what she'd been waiting for.

"Because they don't have a sponsor, Tom. The girls have an adult sponsor who organized the club and everything. Nobody will do it for the guys." Her tone softened a little. She's good.

"Why not?"

"Oh they all think the guys are just a bunch of trouble-makers."

"Aren't they?"

"No!"

"What about that little fight they had the other night when the police had to come break it up?"

"That wasn't our fault!" She exclaimed. "The guard wasn't on the gate and a bunch of outsiders came in and started it."

I couldn't argue with that. "So why don't some of the fathers sponsor the boys?"

"Are you kidding? All they care about is that their kids aren't in the house and they don't get arrested. Other than that, they're on their own."

"Okay, what's this all leading up to, sweetheart?"

"Hunh?" Mock surprise. "What do you mean?"

"I mean what are you really trying to say."

"Well, I just think it's too bad the guys can't find someone to sponsor them. That's all."

"Do you think I should do it?"

"Well…"

"Well I can't."

"Why not?" there was genuine surprise in her voice.

"Because my name isn't on the sales contract, and according to the

30

constitution your mom signed before she bought this place, that's a prerequisite."

"What? You're kidding."

I told her I didn't think so, but I'd check. I got out the ownership papers and the two of us went through them. We finally found the loophole we needed; a clause stating "...owner's representative."

"See? You can do it, Tom!"

"Okay, I'll think about it. Have the guys come over tomorrow and we'll see."

"No way."

""Why not?"

"You might say they're a little paranoid about adults."

We agreed that I'd come down to the corner in front of the community building where they hang out, and she'd introduce me.

From that time on, my life in Middle America became much more interesting. The group she introduced me to was a pretty hard looking collection of junior gangsters. Best word I can think of to describe them would be heterogeneous.

Pete's dad was a Luftwaffe pilot during World War 2, and Pete has trouble handling that. There was Steve, Carl, Jim, Vince and a bunch more – about 20 in the core group with another 20 on the fringes. Almost all of them lived in the complex, but there were a few outsiders. We were worried about the outsiders. Residents could use them as a reason to shoot down what we'd started.

It took a while to establish a level of trust, but we finally ended up with a very cool group. Interesting that my oldest daughter didn't spend much time with them. She was with an entirely different group.

Right after I got together with the young people, my work load dropped off drastically, and I was put "on-call." That meant I only went to work when there was a job, and that became less and less often. So even though I had more time to spend with the young people, our income suffered somewhat. Eventually, I had to start taking free-lance work in the daytime. That meant the kids would be without supervision, so we decided we'd hire a baby-sitter. The oldest girl didn't like that idea, but the others were looking forward to it.

I first saw Connie when I was standing in front of the community center with a couple of the boys. I asked, "Wow. Who's that?"

"Her? That's Connie."

I asked my young friend, "Which one of you guys is going with her?"

"Connie? You're kidding. Hey, man, nobody messes with her."

31

"How come?"

"Aw, I don't know. You just can't get close to her. She's really a cold chick."

The next day I asked my daughter if she knew Connie, and she said she did. I told her to find out if she'd be interested in a baby-sitting job, and if so, arrange for her to come over to the house and talk about it.

Connie did come over a few days later, and we discussed the possibility of her working for us. I asked if she knew anything about us, and she replied, "I've heard of you." indicating nothing. She took the job.

She had a little trouble at first because of the number of teen-age guys hanging around the house. I took care of that by telling all of them, as well as our 3, that when we aren't there, Connie has absolute authority. This gave her a degree of legitimacy that none of the boys had, and she started using it properly in a week.

Connie was 16 when we met, but she seemed much more mature compared to the guys her age. I'm sure a few of the boys had crushes on her, and I couldn't blame them. Pamela and I fell in love with her right away. In fact, she and Pam became close friends after a short period of apprehension on Pam's part. Connie took care of that by making Pam aware of how she felt about me, and that there was nothing romantic or physical.

Connie went to a Catholic high school, so she didn't have day-to-day contact with the other teens in the Complex. It was always interesting to watch the changes in behavior when she walked in the house. All of the normal, macho competitiveness disappeared, and the language softened considerably. It wasn't that she was a prude, but I think they were all afraid of her, thinking she might not come over any more, and that was something none of us wanted.

I spent a lot of time with Connie because she started hanging around when she wasn't working for us. In all the time I was with her, we maintained the roles perfectly; she was the young girl, the daughter, I was the older man, the father. We were never physical with each other until the day I watched her graduate from high school. We hugged and kissed and I was as proud as any father there.

Connie and the other young people hanging around the house afforded me an opportunity to observe them very closely, and I'm sure they were representative of most young people in many ways even though they were individuals. That experience, and what we learned from each other would fill another book, but is not relevant to Sandstone. My dissatisfaction with what I learned in their culture had a lot to do with my reasons for becoming part of the Sandstone Foundation.

Many times after I became part of that, I would flash on how great it would be if those young people could be there with me.

Soon after we moved to Norwalk, we have a house-warming party and I invited a couple I'd known in my roller skating days before I met Pamela. I'd taken the woman to a few concerts with her husband's consent because he hated classical music (why do we marry others who don't share basic values? I have a friend who is a Deadhead, and she admitted that she could never marry a man who wasn't also a deadhead). There had never been a physical relationship between us beyond affectionate hugs and kisses.

During the party I was in the kitchen talking to the woman while her husband was getting another beer, when suddenly Pam walked in and smashed me in the side of the head so hard my ears were ringing.

I managed to get my legs back under me and followed her upstairs where we had a hell of a battle. I finally had to slap her to stop her throwing things at me. I went back downstairs but the party was over.

She apologized the next morning, blaming it on too much booze. I tried to convince her I had no plans to go outside our relationship for anything, especially sex.

A few years later, after I opened a very successful taco shop at the beach, I was awakened early one morning by our oldest daughter who told me in a shaky voice that her mom was downstairs and had cut herself. I thought she meant her mom was fixing breakfast and had an accident.

I got out of bed, still groggy, and started down the stairs when I notice blood-stains on the wall. That woke me up! I hurried down the stairs. When I got to the den I found Pam laying on the couch, wearing ubiquitous panties. She had a wet cloth on one wrist and blood on her hands and arms. She was unconscious. There was also an empty pill bottle on the floor and a note I never did understand except to realize it was a suicide note.

I carried her out to the car and rushed her to the hospital a few blocks away. When we got to the hospital, I called her mom then went through the agony o watching them pump her stomach and sew up the gash on one wrist. She'd come close to succeeding

After they determined she'd live and I'd given a lot of information to the police, she was shipped off to County Hospital and put in the psychiatric ward for a few days.

I spent that night at the beach getting drunk with a few friends and crying a lot. I ended up sleeping on the floor of the taco shop before I locked it up for the last time. It didn't take a genius to figure out she was jealous of it. What I later learned was called Time jealousy.

I talked to Pam's mom the next day and she verified my assessment. Pam hated the taco shop and couldn't stand to work there. All the people made her nervous so she'd drink to make it bearable. But she would usually drink more than enough and became unbearable.

She was finally released into my custody – it's against the law to try and kill yourself – with the stipulation that she undergo psychiatric examination. I took her to the 'shrink' twice, but the second visit was the last. She came out of his office in tears, and I questioned her about it. He had told her not to come back until she was ready to talk about her sex life. She never went back

Looking back, I think I can honestly say the only thing that kept us together was my refusal to admit I'd made another mistake – and my relationship with the children.

A year later, I became associated with the Sandstone Foundation. During that time I was working days for Computer Science Corp. drawing logic diagrams and using a punch-card machine to input them into a computer, and Pamela was working nights. This gave me a lot of time with the children and we became very close. This became even more evident later.

That was my life before Sandstone. I readily plead guilty to being middle-class, chauvinistic, sexually frustrated and more.

Natalie and Me

A few weeks after first meeting John and Barbara, I arrived at the Ranch fairly early to talk to John about a brochure we were going to produce. Since he and Barbara weren't up yet, I decided to go for a swim.

I left my clothes in the closet in the main house, and walked the short distance (which can get very long on cold nights) up to the pool. I opened the sliding glass doors enough to slip in and closed them. The air temperature inside was at least 10 degrees higher than outside, and there were wisps of steam rising off the water. The steam would rise to the ceiling where it would condense and fall back in cold drops that could be a little shocking!

34

I had been paddling around for a few minutes, thoroughly enjoying the warm water on my body, when I heard the sliding glass doors open and close. I turned around to find a very pretty lady putting her towel down on one of the benches. She was nude, and I looked at her with obvious appreciation.

She was in her mid-twenties, somewhat small, but with a beautifully proportioned body that was firm and athletic. Later I learned she was a dance therapist. Her hair was a mass of black curls sitting on top of a rather pixyish face that turned toward me and smiled. "Hi. I'm Natalie." As she spoke, she dropped into the water in the shallow end and rested her arms on the side of the pool.

"Uh…hi. I'm Tom."

"Yes, I've heard of you. You're an artist or something?" What a captivating smile!

"Well, kind of," I hedged. "I'm more of a production artist than what most people consider a real artist."She cocked her head to one side, obviously a little puzzled by that explanation. "What do you mean?"

As she spoke, Natalie started moving slowly over toward where I sat on the steps in the shallow end of the pool. She moved her hands across the surface of the water sensuously, her navel was just visible above the water, her dark bush easily visible just below the surface, and I found myself getting very afraid of this beautiful girl as I tried to explain what a production artist was. God, what a strange sensation! She just might get turned on to me, and I was definitely considering my own reaction watching her approach.

Pamela flashed through my mind. What about her? And our relationship? She'd kill me! Why would she have to know? Hadn't John told me that honesty was one of the most important aspects of their philosophy? Maybe telling Pamela about this little encounter was taking honesty too far!

All I could do was talk…and talk. Faster and faster the closer she got to me. She was turned on!

My arms and hands were kind of floating on the surface, and suddenly her hands were touching mine. She was caressing the backs of my hands and working up my arms. How could I have goose bumps on my skin in this warm water! I felt her knees touch mine. What was I supposed to do?

She'd knelt down until her nipples were just above the surface of the water, and I couldn't take my eyes off them. Then I had to – Her face was only inches away from mine. And I was still talking fast as I could.

She spread her legs far enough apart to wrap them around mine, and was actually sitting on my thighs! Her arms came forward and wrapped around my waist as she finally got as close to me as she could. We kissed. I mean our mouths kissed. Our lips kissed. Our tongues did their mating dance. My mind was spinning off in a hundred different directions, but I was getting one very strong message – I didn't have an erection!

Finally, after a few more minutes of kissing and moving, we separated enough for me to mumble something about the difficulty of getting an erection in the pool, and she did the nicest thing – she agreed with me. She said we should try again sometime on a mattress downstairs. I readily agreed with her and we broke apart.

So that was the first experience I had with a female at Sandstone – and it was a total flop – literally. What the hell happened? I'd never had a problem getting an erection before. Why now?

That wasn't the only time I was impotent, it was just the first. The other times were just as traumatic. I mentioned the problem to John one day.

He laughed softly when I explained it, then said very simply, "Don't worry about it, Tom. Take my word for it, when you really want to have sex with a woman and she wants to have sex with you, you won't have a problem."

When I arrived at the Ranch for one of my early weekday visits, I noticed a number of cars and trucks in the parking lot. John and I were working on the first brochure we planned to publish. Since it was a warm day, I took off my clothes as soon as I entered the house. John and one or two other residents were already nude.

John and I set up office at the dining room table, and started going over the text for the brochure. At some point, a fully-dressed man came upstairs and went out the front door. I asked John about it, and he told me they'd rented the downstairs out to a film company, and they were shooting an X-rated movie. I went back to work on the brochure until a lovely young woman walked through the kitchen and came toward us. She had a white sheet wrapped around her body from neck to ankle. I was just getting ready to smile and say hello when she almost yelled, "For chrissakes! Put some clothes on!" John and I just looked at each other for a moment before the hypocrisy sank in and we laughed softly. The young lady had been downstairs performing all kinds of sex acts in front of a camera, moaning and groaning for the microphones, and she can't handle seeing two grown men casually sitting in the dining room nude? Ridiculous.

A little later, an older woman came toward us, fully dressed, with a nervous little dog prancing along in front of her. John told her, "Lady, there is a large black Manx cat outside that will eat that little puppy for lunch. I suggest you carry it to your car." She quickly grabbed the dog and hugged it to her chest as she hurried out of the house.

At John's suggestion, I went downstairs later, after the crew had left for the day, and discovered that the room was filled with clear plastic inflatable furniture of various colors. Streamers dangled from the ceiling. Obviously a fantasy scene.

Pamela Meets Sandstone

My involvement at Sandstone was sporadic at first, and my visits were confined to the daytime. There were a couple of factors that determined this: Sandstone intimidated me, and I was having a problem making Pamela understand what I was involved in. Since I wasn't sure I understood it, she couldn't share my enthusiasm, and as soon as the word "nudity" came up, she refused to go anywhere near the place.

Not so, though, with the kids. They thought it sounded great, and begged me to take them with me whenever I found an excuse to make the trip.

It was about three months after my first visit to the Ranch before I was able to talk Pamela into going up with me. It was a Tuesday evening, and I picked her up after work. She insisted on stopping at a small beer joint on the way, then we started the hour-long drive with a six-pack rapidly disappearing the closer we got. She was working on the last one as I turned off Topanga Canyon road and started up the hill.

"Shit!"

"What's the matter, Pam?"

"I spilled my beer, damn it. This road is too winding."

"We're almost there." She was beginning to express her nervousness, and the amount of beer she'd drank, and I was having a little trouble hiding mine. I wanted her to like it because it meant so much to me and the kids. We were totally sold on the place and the people – especially the people. Granted, I didn't understand their philosophy, but these people were so beautiful that whatever they were doing had to be right. The relationship between Pamela and me was far from satisfying, and this felt like something that could help bring us closer together.

As I turned off the main road onto the barely paved road and hit the first pothole, she yelled, "My God! Where are you going?"

"This is the entrance road. Not in very good shape. Is it?"

By the time we pulled into the parking lot, it was almost totally dark. This disappointed me a little, because I knew it would have helped if she could have seen the environment in the light. The driveway was lit by a couple of bulbs hanging from the eucalyptus trees, but they did little to light the way to the main house where a porch light made walking much easier.

As I reached for the doorknob, I prayed that the promise I'd made to Pamela would hold up. I'd told her hardly anybody came up on weeknights, so she could be assured of seeing very few people nude. That helped her make up her mind to come with me – that plus the insistence from the kids.

When we entered the living room, I breathed a sigh of relief because the only people present were John and Barbara and Albert. I heard voices from the kitchen, but that turned out to be Dave and Oralia.

I led Pamela over to the couches where they were sitting, and feeling like a girl introducing her boyfriend to her parents, introduced her to them. Of course, John and Barbara had met her when they visited us at the beach.

"Hello, Pamela. It's nice to see you again." Barbara said.

"Hi, Pam. Welcome to Sandstone," Albert added, his eyes moving up and down her body in typical Albert fashion..

She gave him a small, embarrassed smile. "Thank you."

"Hi, Pam. Tom's told us quite a bit about you. I'm glad you finally made it up here," John told her.

The feeling in the room was totally warm and friendly. Most of Pamela's anger and nervousness had been replaced by a very quiet, servile attitude.

Dave and Oralia came out of the kitchen and I made the introductions. They both smiled warmly at her. My nervousness had far from dissipated, even though John and Barbara were the only ones nude. Albert had his shirt off, but Dave and Oralia were fully clothed.

"Why don't you show Pam around, Tom?" Albert suggested.

"Yeah, that's a good idea," I agreed. "Come on, Pam, let me show you the rest of the place."

We got up to leave and Pamela smiled sweetly at them as we moved toward the front door. "Let's go see the pool first."

As we approached the large pool building, I warned her, "Watch out here. There's some steps."

"Okay, I see them."

We got to the sliding glass doors and I pushed them open. "Wait here, Pam, let me turn on…"

Splash!

"…the lights." No! It couldn't happen. I flipped on the lights and turned to the pool. Pamela had walked right into the pool. She was coming up as I got to the edge.

"Pam! Are you okay?"

She was laughing. "I'm okay, Tom. How's that for an introduction?" She started taking off her wet clothes. "Could you get me a robe or something, please?"

I turned and ran out the door, almost tripping on the steps as I turned for the main house and bolted in the front door. "Have you got a bathrobe or something?"

Simultaneously, Albert said, "What happened?" and John said, "In the closet."

"Pam fell in the pool. She didn't hurt herself." I grabbed a terrycloth robe off a hangar and lurched back out the door, hearing Albert's howl of laughter behind me. When I got back to the pool, Pamela was calmly floating around in her panties and bra, seemingly enjoying herself. "Boy, this really feels good."

"I've got a robe for you, Pam, and there's a towel here you can use."

She took her time coming over to the side and climbing out of the warm water. As soon as she felt the cool night air, a big shiver went through her body. "Wow! What a difference."

"Yeah, here, wrap this around you." I handed her the robe. I hadn't noticed before, but the robe was a short one, so when she put it on it exposed quite a bit of her shapely legs. "That's better," I told her, "Let's go back to the house. They have a nice warm fire there."

"Okay, Tom, but what are they going to think?"

"I imagine they're going to think you fell in the pool. They were glad to hear you didn't hurt yourself."

And that's exactly what they did think. We all had a pretty good laugh about the incident – including Pamela.

Oralia came over and told her, "If you give me your clothes, I'll rinse them out and put them in the dryer."

"Oh, I left them on the front porch. I didn't want to get your carpet all wet."

"That's okay," Oralia assured her, "I'll get them." She came back in a few moments with Pamela's clothes. "Where's your underwear?"

In a small, sheepish voice, Pamela told her, "I'm still wearing them."

Oralia said as seriously as she could, "Well, if you give them to me, I'll dry them also."

Pamela managed to remove her underwear without giving anyone the slightest glimpse of anything under that robe. She handed them to Oralia, then sat down by the fire.

"I understand you haven't experienced social nudity before, Pam," John commented after we were all comfortable on the couches again.

"No...never before," she replied in that same small voice.

"Well, don't worry, "John assured her with a smile, "We don't bite...very hard."

It may have been a rather traumatic introduction for the two of us, but it turned out to be a great ice breaker, and we spent the next couple of hours in a very friendly, good-natured conversation.

When her clothes were finally dry, Pamela went in the bedroom and dressed. When she came out, and we were getting ready to go, we all said good night. Pamela made a point of kissing each of the men and at least touching the women. I drove back down the hill in silence, but I think we both felt very good about Pamela's first visit to Sandstone.

Away From Sandstone

Some of the more important experiences I had in those first years didn't happen at Sandstone, but were directly associated with it. For example, Pamela and I had some violent arguments as a result of my visits to the Ranch. I'd come home and immediately be confronted with, "Well...who did you fuck today!" Or if not the actual verbal confrontation, at least the accusing glares and silence that said much the same thing. I'd never seen jealousy so obsessive. A couple of times these confrontations got so bad that it would end up with me calling the Ranch. "Hello, John?"

"Yes."

"John, this is Tom. Hey, I'm sorry, but I just can't handle this anymore. It's tearing our family apart. Pam and I just had a big fight about the whole thing, and the kids are very upset and beginning to take sides. I think it's best if we just forget the whole thing."

"Well, that's up to you, Tom," John would tell me. "You have to do what you feel is best for you."

Why was he so understanding? Why didn't he give me some advice? Anything! I didn't call him to be told I was right.

It was usually less than two weeks before I'd be back at the Ranch. The arguments and phone conversation would never come up unless I brought them up.

There were times when Pamela and I would be at a small party, and the subject of Sandstone would come up. Those times got pretty rough, because it was me against the party. That may sound a little paranoid, but it was true. Very few people expressed positive feelings about what I was doing, and not one of them would accept an invitation to visit the Ranch and see for himself.

Bea asked me, "Who needs it, Tom? I don't have to walk around naked in front of a lot of people to know what I think about nudity." It was a common remark.

"That's true, Bea, but you have to do it to know how you *feel* about it. You have to experience something before you can really make a valid judgment about it."

"Bullshit! I don't have to jump off a building to know how I feel about it." That's a pretty far-fetched analogy, but almost impossible to argue with.

I remember one party of about 20 people, most of them "friends" of ours. Pamela and I had both drank a bit of wine, like everyone else, and the subject was, once again, nudity and Sandstone. Just about everybody there expressed a very liberal viewpoint regarding nudity – it didn't bother them one way or another. At some point during the evening, Pamela and I were standing at the bar with a group of about ten people and someone challenged Pamela about it. To my surprise, she reacted beautifully – she calmly took off everything she was

41

wearing, which consisted of a pair of cut-off jean shorts and a blouse. She'd finally liberated herself from underwear.

Being the only nude person in a room full of people can be upsetting, like being the only dressed person in a room full of naked people. So I quickly followed her example and took off my clothes. It felt really good to see Pamela changing her mind about social nudity at last. The reaction was anything but liberal. About half the people simply left the party, and the rest only stayed long enough to give us some very pointed criticism. Even the host, who'd has his eye on Pamela for a long time, told us he thought our actions were uncalled for. We responded by laughing. We'd made our point about the need to actually experience something, and went home very happy with ourselves.

We talked about the experience later and agreed that Pam's occasional visits to Sandstone, in contrast to her exposure to the pseudo-liberals at the party had been a very important factor in her astonishing behavior that night. She told me not to expect too much from it though, because she was still having trouble accepting the whole concept of open sexuality, and still refused to attend a party with me.

During this time I also took the family to Elysium Fields in Topanga so they could enjoy casual nudity in a social setting with others. I'd met Ed Lange, the founder, before I even knew about Sandstone, and he always greeted me and the family warmly. We also visited Summerland Clothing Optional beach below Santa Barbara.

There was a period from March to October of 1971 when we had very little contact with Sandstone. We'd leased a 40-acre ranch in the wilderness of Trancas Canyon in Malibu, north of Point Dume. There was no running water, except the small creek until it dried up, no electricity and no gas. There were just two dilapidated tin shacks that were having trouble remaining upright in one of the most beautiful settings in the Santa Monica Mountains. We were kept so busy just surviving that we had little time to visit others.

Before that, we had been living in a beautiful, old, two-story house in Manhattan Beach, dividing our time between earning money and helping to publish an underground newspaper called "The Beach Peoples' Easy Reader."

The paper started out as a real "fun" thing that gave me a good format to express my opinions about our philosophy, but it got a little scary later when we started uncovering some unsavory things going on at City Hall, especially in the police department. At one point the police wanted to shut me up so badly that I had to go to Sandstone for a few days to keep from being arrested before I presented some facts to the City manager's office.

It was during this same time that my thirteen year-old daughter came to me and asked if we could talk. "Sure. What's on your mind?"

"Well, I've got to give a speech in my English class next week, and I want to do it on nudism. Will you help me?"

She was a freshman at the local high school which was not known for its liberal outlook, even though it was a 'beach' school. We both knew there might be some interesting reactions to such a speech, and I was very proud of her for making the decision. We discussed some of the problems she might face and the best way to present the subject. We borrowed a couple of very dry technical books on social nudism from the Sandstone library and started doing the research.

"Okay, Tom, I've got all this information on three-by-five cards and know what I'm going to say, but how do I start it?"

"Well, sweet, you have two choices: either you stand up in front of the class and take your clothes off, or you start by saying 'I'm a nudist and this is why.'" Fortunately, she chose the latter.

The speech was such a success that she got A on the assignment, and a week later when the teacher asked the class what subject they wanted for a debate, they unanimously chose nudism.

My daughter and a boy were selected to represent the PRO side, and two other boys were selected for the CON side. She brought her partner home and introduced him to me. As the two of them spent more time working together on the debate, it became obvious that there was a very good relationship developing.

They were working one evening and they asked my advice on a point. During the discussion she said, "Don't you think it would help I we took him up to Sandstone and let him actually experience nudism?"

"Sounds like a good idea." I asked the boy if he'd like to do that.

"Uh…sure, Tom. Sounds like a great idea." Part of his enthusiasm was probably based on the fact that my daughter had a great body, and the possibility of seeing her nude had some bearing on it.

"Okay, first of all, we need a signed note from your parents saying they understand where you'll be going and they give their permission. Can you get that for me?"

"Yeah, I think so. It's part of my homework."

I told my daughter to get a brochure that he could take home.

We didn't see him for a while, and I finally asked her if we were going to take him with us.

"No," she said simply.

"How come?"

"His folks won't give him permission."

"That's too bad. Are you disappointed?'

"Yeah, kinda. They just about lost a son by not doing it."

"That's too bad."

She said nothing more, but I knew the experience had a big effect on her.

You might ask why we just didn't let him join us in casual nudity at our home, and the reason is the same; his parents would have to agree to it or we could get in big trouble.

A week later, she came home from school an hour after leaving. I asked why, and she laughed. Said she got sent home for not wearing a bra.

First, I went up to the school and told them what I thought of their dress code, then I pulled my daughter out of that school and enrolled her in a Special Education school. They didn't care what the students wore because they got paid for attendance.

Pat and Bea

There was one warm day in the summer of 1971 when we did manage to coerce two of our friends, Pat and Bea, into coming up to Sandstone with us – a lot of the coercing came from the children. At the time, Sandstone had a "Family Day" the last Sunday of the month. It allowed the members a chance to bring their families up to the Ranch for the day, so all of us, plus Pat and Bea, drove up the mountain to spend a lovely day at Sandstone.

The children were very excited about Pat and Bea coming with us, because they always enjoyed introducing people to their new love. Brandi was the most avid Naturist in the family, and once in a while Carrie Lynn complained about Brandi being nude when she brought her girlfriends home, but I think it was mostly just talk. Secretly, I think Carrie Lynn enjoyed seeing her friends' reaction to how comfortable Brandi was walking around nude.

At Sandstone, it was a different story. Carrie couldn't wait to get her clothes off. The oldest, was reluctant to 'go all the way' so she usually wore the bottom of her bikini, even on the hottest days.

Pat and Bea seemed to enjoy themselves that day, and met some nice people they talked with at length, but never took their clothes off. I take that back...Pat did take his off when he went in the swimming pool with the children. Bea spent the whole day bundled up in a long skirt, long-sleeved blouse, and even a hat.

I watched Bea the whole time she was there, and she seemed to really enjoy sitting on the front lawn talking to people – even though she was fully dressed and they were nude. Finally, late in the day, I had a chance to be alone with her for a few minutes. "Bea, I realize I told you everything was completely optional here, I must admit to some frustration at your refusal to try social nudity. Can you explain?"

"Tom, I feel that if I take my clothes off, I'll be waving a red flag in front of all these guys that I want to have sex with them."

I laughed gently, "Oh, I don't think they'll get that impression. There are a lot of other women going nude, and I can assure you they don't feel that way. Maybe it would just take a few minutes to get used to it."

"But you don't understand. I think I do want to have sex with them – at least a few of them."

She went home that evening without experiencing social nudity, but she did discover how closely she associated nudity with sex.

I Move In

When I finally took the big step and moved to Sandstone, the family had gone through many changes. Of the original five I'd met, only John and Barbara were still there.

Dave and Oralia had moved out; Frank and Terri moved in and out; Cristen and Jaime had moved in and been told to move out; Albert had also been told to leave. Those were the only three people I know of who were told to leave Sandstone.

Marty and Mag had moved in, and Mag moved out. Most of this activity took place while we were living in the wilds of Trancas Canyon, so I'm not sure of the details. Albert came to visit us occasionally, and cried on our shoulders about everything that was happening. Of course his views were strictly subjective, and prejudiced by problems he was having with John and Barbara – he was trying to buy the Ranch.

Also during that period, Stephen Beltz and his family arrived in their big, yellow school bus, and took up temporary residence on the "high site." They, too, left before I arrived.

That doesn't mean I had no contact with those members of the family; on the contrary, we had quite a bit of contact with all of them at different times. From the first visit to Sandstone until we moved to Trancas, Dave and Oralia were two of my favorite people, and I welcomed any opportunity to be with them. Dave was almost as physically beautiful as Oralia, but he didn't scare me like she did. Her beauty plus her attitude and bearing were overwhelming.

On Saturday nights the family prepared a gourmet dinner for those members who would pay extra for it. It was usually served about eight P.M. Dave and Oralia would not appear at the house until just minutes before dinner, and their entrance was always met with great interest by both the males and the females – they were both very desirable people. I must admit I was never aware of them having any sexual contact with the members, but that's not to say they didn't; my attendance at the parties was rare, and my visits downstairs even rarer.

I did have an opportunity to talk to Dave several times when I went up during the day, and he filled me in on some of the background before they moved to the Ranch – fantastic stories about sixteen-hour encounter sessions every day for weeks at the house in the San Fernando Valley.

Frank and Terri were probably the two family members I knew least (though Frank became very important to us after Sandstone closed). This was primarily due to the fact that they were the only members of the family who continued working their day jobs in the city. So they weren't there when I went up.

Marty and Mag were the youngest members of the family, and the couple Pamela and I knew best. The four of us would go for long walks at night and listen to all of nature's nocturnal sounds.

Once they suggested that Pamela and I spend the night with them in their cottage – we quickly declined. On the way home, we both realized how paranoid our decision was; no one had even mentioned sex, but we discovered we got scared off by even the thought of it. To our knowledge, we were the only two even thinking about it. Neither Marty or Mag had intimated anything more than saving us a long drive down the mountain at night.

I had met Cristen and Jaime before they moved to Sandstone in conjunction with an underground paper a friend of theirs wanted me to help publish. I wasn't too impressed with them at first, nor their friend, and was surprised to see they had moved to the Ranch. Jaime was a nice, young lad who seemed to have an identity crisis, and Cristen appeared to be a very strong female who gave me the impression she'd stomp on anyone who got in her way.

The Beltz family didn't arrive at Sandstone until my family had given up on civilization, so I didn't meet them until one of my later visits. I did know of Steve, because he had written the original prospectus on the Foundation (The Sandstone foundation for Community systems Research, Inc.), and I'd worked on that.

Steve and Judith and their five children had nothing but trouble at the Ranch. According to Steve, part of it had to do with the open sexuality, and part with the children. The Sandstone environment was not designed to accommodate children; the legal questions made the situation difficult.

I'm really not sure why all of this happened – why all those people came and went.

I never had a chance to question them about it, but there were a lot of rumors flying around. For example, Albert told us Dave and Oralia left because of irreconcilable differences with Marty., but he wouldn't elaborate. From what he did tell us, it was obvious that there was no love lost between him and Marty, so it was difficult to put too much value on his information. The story I got from

47

John and Barbara was completely different and indicated a reluctance on Dave and Oralia's part to work through an impasse they'd come up against.

Dave and Oralia did visit us in Trancas, but they gave no reason for their leaving, they only expressed a profound disillusionment with John and Barbara. I couldn't put too much credence in that, though, because most people found it necessary to make Sandstone or the Williamsons out to be wrong rather than confront their own inability to cope with the pressures placed on them by the environment.

I do know that Albert tried to set up a corporation involving some of the members for the purpose of buying the Ranch, and that his behavior became very negative when the deal fell through. I'm not sure Albert ever understood what Sandstone was really all about. His primary function was to run the club, Sandstone Retreat, and he did that very well from what I could see. One of his most important attributes was that he was completely non-threatening to any of the men who brought their mates to the parties. Nobody took Albert too serious; he was a self-proclaimed Swinger. The sexual activity he participated in could only be called "recreational sex." Actually, he did some men a favor by helping females make the transition to Sandstone.

He was at his best with women who came to the Retreat not knowing too much about it, or only came as their partner's "ticket" to the party. He could make them feel very comfortable in a short time, and he also ran interference for their mates once in a while; if he knew some guy was busy downstairs, and his wife might get upset by it, Albert would spend time with the woman to make things easier all around.

When his plan to buy Sandstone started looking shaky, he called some of the members and asked them not to pay their membership dues in an effort to force the Williamsons into a position where they would have to sell. It didn't work, and the scheme was an important factor in his leaving.

As for Cristen and Jaime, I don't know what happened, but I'd heard they were trying to "use" Sandstone for their own financial benefit, rather than working for the whole community.

I consider myself very fortunate in having the opportunity to be at Sandstone when the family consisted of John and Barbara, Dave and Oralia, Frank and Terri and Albert.

Pamela and I and the children were very busy trying to survive in Trancas during that time, and we just couldn't keep up with all the changes. John was a big help to us, though, giving us a water tank that wasn't being used at the Ranch, and a lot of basic information about survival.

It was when we lived in Trancas Canyon that Brandi admitted her interest in other females. Specifically, she was very attracted to her high school gym coach and had received some encouragement – or at least she thought she had. I didn't consider her bisexuality that unusual, considering her exposure to casual nudity at home and during her visits to the Ranch; it gave her more exposure to the naked bodies. Also, she'd listened to me talk about the Sandstone philosophy regarding sexuality a number of times.

Later, Pamela packed the family in a van and took off across the country. Then Brandi showed up at the Ranch one day. She'd gotten tired of her mom's trip, which included an 18-year old boy toy, and had hitch-hiked back to Malibu. She told me she only had to perform two sex acts all the way from Texas. She lived with me in the cabin for a short time before moving back to the beach.

It was also during this period that John secluded himself in the bedroom and refused to come out for about ten days. That was shortly after Dave and Oralia left, but I'm not sure the two events were connected. When we went up to the Ranch, people would tell us to be careful around John because of his mood, but he was never anything but pleasant to all of us.

Pamela and I finally went our separate ways in October of 1971. I moved out of Trancas, and rented a small bachelor apartment in Hermosa Beach, and she left the canyon about a month later. The breakup was amicable, and we continued seeing each other occasionally. I went back to work as a free-lance graphic artist, and she got her job back as a typist.

Later that month, I was spending more time at the Ranch working on a graphic project than I was in my own apartment. There was a lovely lady named Sondra living there, and we spent a few nights sharing a bed. Finally, after four straight days there, I asked John if I could put a mattress in the small office under the north house and live there full time. His answer was almost too simple. "Well, you're here. What else is there to talk about?"

Finally, I was going to become part of the family.

As I said before, the family had changed during my eight months living in Trancas. John and Barbara were still there, now living in an Executive motorhome they'd purchased to facilitate their increased traveling (Where did they get the money for that!). Marty was still there but without Mag. She'd left the previous summer, and he was now occupying the master bedroom in the main house.

Butch and Sherri, who had been members before John invited them to move in, were living in the north house. Sondra was living in the west house with her daughter, Jaime, and Jaime's boyfriend Anders. Michael and Janice were living in the cottage.

The office I moved into had no bathroom or kitchen. All I did there was work and sleep. I used the bathroom facilities in the pool building, and ate meals in the main house with the rest of the family.

So the family numbered eleven. That was the largest it had ever been, and stretched the physical capacity to its limit. To make things even more difficult, I awoke one morning to find another couple eating breakfast in the main house.

Tutt and Marcia had met the Williamsons when they'd parked the motorhome in Arizona, and simply started a conversation with them. Tutt and Marcia said they were headed for Los Angeles, and John told them to get in touch if they had a problem finding a place to stay. He hadn't bothered to tell them anything about Sandstone, and the first thing they saw when they pulled into the parking lot was somebody walking by nude. Marcia, more than Tutt, was a little uptight, so she just about freaked out before they'd gotten parked.

In the months they lived with us, I don't think I saw either of them nude more than three times. It was a good example of a circular trip; she was afraid of what he might do if she opened up, and he was afraid of what she might do if he did. Individually, they both expressed interest in our lifestyle, but were reluctant to take an active role in it. Physically, they were both good-looking, but they didn't believe it. Marcia was continually putting herself down, and any attempt to boost her low self-esteem was met with suspicion – "Stop it, I know what you want," she would say, but with a look that said, "And if you keep trying you may get it." I gave up trying.

First Party

I was sitting on the floor, naked, my back against the wall, my butt resting on the deep, plush, brilliant red carpeting, my knees drawn up as close to my chest as I could get them, my arms wrapped tightly around them to make sure they didn't slip, my eyes trying to follow the dozens of other naked people walking casually around the large room. And I was scared to death! And paralyzed! Oh, my God! That couple over there…on the mattress. Are they…really…yup! They sure are! Am I supposed to watch that???

I mean, I helped John write the text for the first brochure advertising the private club, Sandstone Retreat, and it sounded pretty banal at the time. This is not banal! This is a real-life Fellini movie in Cinerama and I'm the only spectator!

No…wait. That pretty lady over there seems to be just watching. I mean, she's standing up for one thing. And she looks like she's watching that couple…oh, oh. She just looked over here.

She's…coming…this way. "Hi."   Try to sound suave!

"Hello." It's like I have Jiminy Cricket on my shoulder talking to me. Can she see him?

"Can I join you?"

"Uh…sure. Please…have a seat. I mean…" Where did the high-pitched voice come from! Hey, Jiminy, can't you do any better than that???

She sits down next to me. Too close!

"Thanks. I'm Rhonda."

"Hello, Rhonda, I'm…uh…Tom." How could I forget my own name!

"Hi, Tom. How come you're sitting over here alone? If you don't mind me asking."

"No…no, not at all…Rhonda. I just…came downstairs, and thought I'd…"

"Just watch?"

"Um…yes, that's it. Weren't you watching…that…couple…over there?"

"Yes. That lady is really pretty!" she said.

"Well, uh…so are you." Not even close to suave!

"Thanks, but not like her. That's my husband she's with."

"Your…husband." Is it getting warm in here? I'm sweating!

"Yes."

51

Try to sound scholarly. Thanks, Jiminy. "Um, how do you feel about that?"

"Well. This is our first time here, and the first time I've…you know…seen him…"

"Yes?"

"Do you just want to talk, Tom?"

"Uh…well, yes…I guess so…right now. What else did you…?"

"Oh, nothing. Really. I'd just like to talk to someone. That is if you're not busy…you know."

"No…I'm not…busy." Define busy! I'm almost peeing in my pants – if I was wearing any!

"Where's your wife?" she asked.

"My…wife…? Oh, she's home."

"Oh, I thought the club was for couples."

"Well, it is, but I…uh, I work for Sandstone, so I'm an exception."

Oh, God! She put her hand on my leg!

"You work here?"

"Well…uh, not exactly here…I mean, we live down at the beach, but I come up here…"

"Wow! That must be exciting! What do you do?"

"Rhonda, would you mind if we went upstairs and talked?" In other words, how the hell am I supposed to have an intelligent conversation sitting here in the middle of an orgy!

"Oh, that would be great! Can we get a glass of wine?"

"Definitely!" How about a whole bottle!

"Swell," she patted my leg!

"Jerry looks like he's having a problem, so it could take a while."

She stood up, and I tried. If I lean against the wall, I think I'll make it. I wasn't going to get into Jerry's problem.

We made our way upstairs, I followed her up the carpeted staircase with my eyes glued to her amazingly swaying butt. We stopped in the kitchen long enough to get two glasses of wine from a bottle I brought, then went in the dining room and sat on the floor with our backs against the divider. When I looked at her, I realized she was much prettier than what I'd seen in the dim light downstairs. And I felt much more comfortable up here…even with a lovely nude woman sitting beside me – for the first time. This night is filled with firsts!

After we both took a sip of the wine, she asked, "So what do you do?"

"What do I…"

She giggled, "For Sandstone, Tom."

"Oh, of course. Sorry…"

"That's okay. I have the same problem," she admitted.

"Problem? What problem?" Like I didn't know! It's even warmer up here!

"You know, trying to talk about anything but…uh, sex here."

"Oh, that. Well, the environment is conducive…" She has very lovely nipples. Small, well-formed breasts, just what I like

She nudged me. "Come on, what do you do?"

"Yes, right. Well, I'm a writer and a production artist." And I think I'm falling in love!

"Okay, I know what writers do, but what do production artists do?"

"We put all the pieces together, the text, photos, artwork, into a finished publication." That actually sounded intelligent. This is much better.

"That's interesting. And you're doing that for Sandstone?"

"Yes, we're finishing up work on the first brochure."

"That's nice. Can I see it?"

"No, sorry. Not yet. I sent it to the printers today." Oh, sure I did! Maybe in two weeks.

"Oh, too bad. I'd like to see what it says."

"Why?"

"Well…Jerry, my husband, didn't really tell me much about the place before we got here. It was kind of a shock. All those naked people…"

"Yes, I can imagine. Are you and Jerry nudists?"

"Ha! No way! He doesn't even want the kids to see me in panties and a bra! Which I think is kind of silly since that covers me more than my bikini. I've thought about visiting a nude beach, but Jerry…"

"Well, then I can imagine…and then downstairs…but you do have the right idea about casual family nudism. It can really bring the family closer together."

"That's nice to know. Thanks. I'll give it a try – no matter what Jerry says."

She reached over and put her hand on my leg – again. I was never so aware of another person's touch. "Can I…be honest…with you, Tom?"

"I certainly hope so, Rhonda."

She took more than a sip of wine. Almost time to go get the bottle.

"Well, Jerry went downstairs before me. I was kind of stuck…didn't know what to do."

Suddenly, our shoulders and thighs were touching. And our feet! "But he told me where he was going, so I found my way down there."

"And?" Did I just feel movement…down there? Not now!

"I couldn't believe it! People all over the room, doing all kinds of things!"

"Yes," I agreed, "It can be a little overwhelming." What an understatement!

"Well…probably not for you since you work here, but me…wow." Oh, if she only knew! "Anyway, I didn't see Jerry at first, the light was so dim. Then I recognized him on that mattress with that pretty lady."

"I think I asked you downstairs how you felt when you saw them."

"Yes, you did. And I didn't know how to answer you. I still don't."

"I assume you've never seen Jerry with…"

"Gawd no!"

"Kind of a shock?"

"Slightly! But then I started watching them like…you know…just two people…I mean, I've seen porno movies before. Jerry uses them to…you know…"

"And?"

"And I was kind of okay with it until…"

"Until what?"

"Until the lady looked at me and winked. Then she motioned me toward them with her hand." This was getting much too complicated, and we were both out of wine. I excused myself, and went in the kitchen. I returned a few minutes later with the bottle and poured more in both glasses.   She took a long drink, then started talking faster. "At first, I wasn't sure what she meant…I mean, I've never been with a…woman, so…I didn't want to…."

"That must have been when I noticed you. You weren't moving."

"No," she admitted. "You know what they say about a rock and a hard place…"

Did she have to use that metaphor!!! Or is it a simile? Who cares!

She thought a long moment, took another drink. "Okay, Tom, you said I could be honest with you."

"Please. Be honest."

"Okay. At first…I was…stunned, I guess is a good word. Then I kind of took inventory, and was very surprised to find out that I was excited…turned on…by her."

"Wonderful!"

54

"Yes, it was. Like I said, I've never…been with a woman, but I still didn't know what to do. I mean, I could see Jerry was having his usual problems, so I didn't want to…" Her leg was moving against mine.

"Do you think he knew you were there?"

"No way. His head was buried in her hair."

"So that's when you came over to me?"

"Right," she stroked my leg. More movement! "I saw you when I came downstairs, and you looked…lonely. Which I thought was pretty weird considering…where we were…and what was… "

"Well…I wasn't exactly lonely, but…"

"So I came over to meet you." She leaned over and kissed my cheek. "And I'm glad I did."

I leaned over and kissed the side of her neck. "Thank you. So am I."

She moaned softly, and murmured, "Oh, don't do that. I am so…what… sensitive right now."

"Why not?"

"Because…that's a big…red…button when you kiss me there."

I leaned over and whispered in her ear, "And what happens if I push the button?" Definite movement!

She took a drink of wine. "You'd better be ready for the consequences."

"I'm ready, Rhonda. What about you?"

This time she didn't kiss my cheek. Our lips met, parted, our tongues did their dance. I moved the wine bottle and glasses out of the way and slid down until we were laying next to each other. "Uh, Tom, don't you want to go downstairs?"

I nuzzled her neck. "What for?"

"Well…I mean…we're right here…"

"Are you uncomfortable?"

"Oh, no! I've never been so comfortable!"

"Then let's stay here."

And we did.

Another first – for both of us. We made love in front of other people. Or we did if anyone happened to walk by. Personally, a hundred piece marching band could have gone by playing the Notre Dame fight song and I wouldn't have known it, because it was also the first time I've been so totally into my partner. This was a whole new level of sexuality I didn't even know existed.

55

Freakout!

It wasn't too long after my move to Sandstone that I had my freakout.
It happened when I came face-to-face with one of the biggest problems people had to handle at Sandstone – the green-eyed monster, JEALOUSY.

John and I talked about it a few times, and his feeling was that jealousy, as most people perceive it, isn't real. He was talking about possessive jealousy, the kind that can eat your guts out, and lead to violent reactions. He felt it wasn't real because it was based on an ownership principle, and no person owns another person. Actually, that type of jealousy is a Fear – the fear of loss, fear of inadequacy, etc. If a person looks at his feelings from that perspective, it is much easier to work on the fear.

John does feel that there are two types of jealousy that are real; Time Jealousy and Selectivity Jealousy. Let me explain: Time Jealousy; "I don't mind who you're with or what you're doing, but you've been out of my space too long." Selectivity Jealousy; "I don't care what you're doing or how long you've been gone, but I don't approve of the person you're with. He (or she) doesn't measure up to my standards."

Obviously, these are over-simplified descriptions of a complex problem, but they will suffice for the sake of this discussion. Time Jealousy can be handled by a simple phone call. Selectivity Jealousy requires open, honest communication in the relationship – which should be there anyway.

In my case, I'd gone down to the city one Saturday morning to get a small job printed, and decided to stop off and see how Pamela and the children were doing while the job was getting printed. Pamela brought up Sandstone. "Are you having a party tonight?"

"Sure, Pam," I told her. "We have one every Saturday night. It's our 'reeelee beeg night," I told her laughingly in my worst Ed Sullivan impersonation.

"Oh, yeah, that's right. How about taking me back up with you then bringing me home tomorrow sometime?"

I had to think about that for a second. I must admit I enjoyed my time at Sandstone without Pamela, and I wasn't sure her presence might change my behavior. But she'd never asked to attend a party before. "Sure. That sounds like a great idea."

From the other side of the room, her daughter asked, "Can I come, too?"

I explained to her that she wouldn't be able to come down to the main house or even the swimming pool, but if she wanted to come with those restrictions, it was up to her mother.

Pamela said, "Sure. Why not!"

The three of us got back to the Ranch about five o'clock after I picked up the printing job, and her daughter went straight to the west house where there was a TV, and where she would sleep. It was also where Jaime and Anders were, and I knew the three of them had developed a close relationship. Pamela and I went to the main house where we were warmly greeted by the rest of the family and a few early arriving members.

One of those was supposedly an architect named Ron. He and I didn't get along too well, mainly because he never brought anyone with him. He said he was doing some drawings for us on improvements, but we hadn't seen any results yet. He always picked party nights to come up and talk business with Barbara.

I had mentioned to Barbara that I'd been asked by a couple of members what right he had to be there alone when they were required to bring dates, but she only said, "He's my guest." Telling her about the feedback I'd gotten didn't help. He was her guest, and whether he was using Sandstone to fulfill his own neurotic needs or not, her decision stood.

But, the reader might ask, what about Pamela being there as a single female – since I would be working. Good question. Simply put, we had found that one or two single females did not disturb the dynamics of a party, but just one single male could, and usually did, cause problems. The great majority of female members (or partners of members or even guests) were not intimidated by another female. The same could not be said for the males.

Pamela and I had gone downstairs to play some pool, and Ron followed us. He started giving her his line – showing her drawings of modern igloos for a housing project in Alaska that never got built, a school that also never got built, and running up and down the stairs to fill her wine glass as soon as she emptied it – which was much too often.

As you can see, I was already getting uptight. Pamela and I had never had sex downstairs, and my plan was to leave shortly after dinner and go back to my

57

office where we could make love. It disturbed me to see her buying this guy's line – Selectivity Jealousy.

There's another element to this story, and I have to backtrack to explain it. About a week before this particular Saturday night, I met a young woman who was interviewing Marty. Her name was Melinda, and she was an anthropology student from UCLA. She'd heard about Sandstone from another student, and was looking for someone she could do an in-depth interview with. I asked her what the interview was for, and she replied in a very soft, sweet voice that her paper was going to be on a person leading a completely different lifestyle from her own.

Marty had already dismissed her and was doing something else (which means he didn't score), so I asked if she'd like to walk up to the office and talk about it. She agreed, and we left the main house.

As we walked up the driveway, I noticed she was taller than I first thought, about five-seven or –eight. She was wearing a long, thin, print dress that covered her from neck to ankle, but left no doubt what was underneath it – and it wasn't underwear. Her dark hair wasn't too long, and she had freckles that made her look younger than her twenty-seven years. All in all, I was impressed.

We sat in the office about an hour, and Melinda asked some very good questions about our lifestyle and what made it so unique. I tried to explain it by comparing our value system with hers, but she had trouble understanding that. "Okay, Melinda, look at it this way. I'm sitting here nude which should indicate where I put nudity in my value system."

"What do you mean?"

"Well, if I was living in your environment, with your value system, I might have a bit of trouble walking around naked. So what I did was find an environment where I could go nude anytime I felt like it, because I value that freedom."

"Why?" she asked. "What's so important about running around without your clothes?"

I thought a minute. "It feels good! But more importantly, it doesn't matter whether I go nude or wear clothes, I do both, but what's important is that I can go nude if I feel like it. And you're never going to find out what that's all about until you experience it."

58

She looked at me a long time before replying, "I think I'll pass on that – for the time being."

"That's too bad, Melinda."

"Why do you say that?"

I smiled, "Because I think you'd look very good nude, and I also think you'd enjoy it." I was looking straight into her eyes when I said this, and she finally had to duck her head to avoid my gaze.

She came back up twice that week, and we talked for hours each time, and each time I had more trouble keeping my mind on the conversation. Finally, toward the end of the second interview, I told her how I felt. "Melinda, I want to make love to you."

"What!" she exclaimed. I didn't think it would catch her that far off guard. I'd been giving plenty of signals up to now, but I assume she wasn't reading them.

"I said, 'I want to make love to you.' In fact, I'd say it's going to be difficult for me to continue talking to you if we don't make love."

"Why? What's the matter?"

"Nothing is the matter. It's just that it's getting very difficult for me to be with you, looking at you, smelling you but not touching you. You turn me on. Is there something wrong with that?"

"No," she replied, "I don't think there's anything wrong with people having sex, but..."

"But what? You're putting out signals that the thought has crossed your mind."

"Well..."

"Well what?"

"Well, right now I'm on my period."

59

"I don't give a damn about your period!"

"Well, I do," she replied defensively. "So…let's just wait a while and see how we feel later."

I laughed, "If that isn't an example of different value systems, I don't know what is."

That ended the interview for the day.

I didn't see Melinda again until she showed up at the party I'd brought Pamela to. She arrived just before dinner, and that just added to my confusion. She came in wearing another long dress, but left the room shortly after arriving, and returned a few minutes later, nude like the rest of us.

"Hey, fantastic!" I told her. "I thought I was never going to see that body." And I'd been right – it was a body worth seeing. Not spectacular, but definitely pleasing. She came over and sat on the floor between Pamela and me, Ron was sitting on the other side of Pamela, and working hard to keep her attention on him.

Melinda leaned against me and whispered, "I feel a little weird, about the string I mean."

"What string?" I asked absently, enjoying the touch of our bodies.

"You know, the string on my Tampax."

"Oh, Christ! Don't sweat the little things. Lots of women wear them every month. Some of them are really in their period."

"What's that supposed to mean?" She was defensive again.

"Come on, Melinda, don't take it the wrong way, I'm sure you're in your period. I was just commenting that some women wear them when they're not – so they have an easy cop-out for not getting involved with anyone."

Melinda's look changed from defensive to puzzled. "I don't understand."

"Oh. Well, I try and explain it later. Right now, it's time to eat." Ron and Pamela had already headed for the dining room, so I helped Melinda up and we joined them. After we'd filled our plates with food, the four of us returned to sit on the living room floor.

At some point, Pamela leaned over and asked me, "Who's your little friend?"

"Oh, Melinda? I introduced you to her. She's a student at UCLA doing research on a paper she's writing for a Sociology class."

"Have you fucked her yet?" Pamela always made that word sound very dirty.

"No, I haven't," I replied.

"Uh huh. Well, I bet you'd like to." There was venom in her voice, and when I looked at her she was glaring at me. I didn't respond.

After dinner, Ron intensified his attack on Pamela, and she intensified her attack on the wine bottle. I tried having a conversation with Melinda, but it didn't work. I was getting more uptight by the minute. I did keep talking to Melinda, but only to keep her near me. At one point, she asked if she could have a cup of coffee, and I offered to get it for her. As I got up to go to the kitchen, Pamela got up and walked a few feet in front of me.

While I was filling the coffee cups, Pamela went over to the refrigerator and poured herself another glass of wine. She got a couple of ice cubes out of the freezer. As she walked toward me, she took an ice cube out of her glass and rubbed it slowly down my chest. "Sorry, he turns me on," she told me. Her look was almost triumphant.

"What are you sorry about?"

She walked past me without answering.

I returned to the living room, and gave Melinda her coffee. As I resumed my seat next to her, I noticed Ron had progressed to putting his arm around Pamela's waist. She moved a little closer so his arm encircled her even more. I was distracted when Melinda spoke. "Tom, tell me what you meant about women wearing Tampax."

"Oh, that. All I meant was that it isn't too uncommon for females to use that as a cop-out for not getting involved in the activity downstairs. They know a lot of guys are reluctant to have sex with a woman when she's in her period. Also, a lot of women don't like to have sex when they're in their period, so it works both ways."

"Well, it can get a little messy, you know." She seemed almost apologetic.

Ron's deep, slightly slurred voice interrupted us. "Hey, we're going for a swim. Want to join us?"

I turned to Melinda. "You want to?"

"Sure. Why not. You have a towel I can borrow?"

"They're in the closet," I told her as we got up. I opened the closet door, and heard Pamela say, "Tom, get me a towel, too. I didn't bring one, but I've sure left enough of them up here." She, like a lot of people, left many items at Sandstone, but towels were at the top of the list. Panties ran a close second.

I grabbed three towels, and the four of us walked up to the pool building. There were already six or eight people in the water, most of them just leaning

61

against the sides or walking around in the warm, shallow water. Very few people actually swam in that pool.

I put the towels on a bench, and Melinda and I followed Pamela and Ron down the steps into the water. The three of us started walking away, but Melinda sat on the steps. Pamela paddled around a bit, and ended up on the seat built into the side in the deep end. Ron took a longer route to end up beside her. I swam a fast lap and joined Melinda on the steps. "Is something bothering you, Tom?"

I wasn't sure what I wanted to tell her, but I said, "Yeah, I'm having a little trouble handling this trip, so do me a favor and stay close. Okay?"

"Sure," she replied, "But hasn't this happened before?"

"Not really. Pam has always been reluctant to relate to another guy before tonight, and I'm not sure exactly what she's doing now." What was happening was that Ron and Pamela had left the deep end of the pool and were now standing in shallow water embracing. I felt my stomach do a flip-flop.

One of the women in the pool came up behind me and put her arms around my chest. I felt her body mold itself to mine. "Come on, Tom. Let me float you." She started pulling me away from the steps, but I wasn't in the mood for it, and wasn't sure how Melinda would react.

"Sorry, Lynn, I'm not in the mood right now."

"Wow, you feel really tight. I'm sorry too. Maybe later." She moved away, but I couldn't get my mind off what the two of them were doing only feet away. Melinda tried to talk to me, but gave up when I didn't respond. I even tried a few moves with her, we kissed and I slid my hands up her legs, but it wasn't working, and I knew she wasn't going to change her mind about having sex while she was menstruating. Actually, I'm not even sure I was capable of it.

Finally, I couldn't stand the torture anymore, mumbled something to Melinda and got out of the water. I walked back to the main house, not even feeling the evening chill, and walked inside. It's impossible to describe the painful, empty feeling in my stomach. I also felt very confused. I couldn't make any logical decisions about my behavior, and all the talks John and I had about their philosophy raced through my head.

I was standing in front of the fireplace, getting warm, when I saw Ron and Pamela walk up the porch. But instead of coming in the house, they went in the side door which led to the kitchen – and the stairs going down. That did it! Now I could act…I could get the hell out of there.

I walked, stumbled and ran up to the office. It was the only place I felt secure – to some degree. And there were no people in the office. I couldn't handle people. I sat down at the desk and looked at a drawing I was working on, but I wasn't able to focus on it. My mind was too confused to concentrate on anything. I turned on the radio – and immediately turned it off. I couldn't handle the noise.

I couldn't sit still, but the office didn't have enough room for me to walk around, so I went outside. That was a little better. The night was cool and quiet with just a hint of noise emanating from the main house and the swimming pool. This was a party night. It felt good to have room to walk, but my legs weren't too cooperative. I had to consciously put one foot in front of the other to move.

I'm not sure how I got there, but I found myself in front of the West House. I knew that Sondra and Pam's daughter were sleeping in there, the other two had gone down the hill. I felt I had to talk to someone who would have some idea of what I was going through, so I went in.

They must not have been sleeping very long, if at all, because they both came into the living room when I entered.

"What's up, Tom?" Sondra asked through a yawn.

"I'm having a little trouble."

The girl asked, "What do you mean?"

So I tried to tell them what was happening, or at least what I thought was happening, down at the party. The more I talked, the more trouble I had talking until I ended up lying beside the couch shaking. I thought I was going to vomit any minute.

They both knew what I was going through, and they also knew there was really nothing they could do or say to make it better. They tried, but they knew it was hopeless.

I stayed on the floor a few minutes, and when I felt like my body would support me again, I got up to leave. "Shit! This isn't doing any of any good. I'll see you later."

Sondra said, "Tom, I'm sorry. I wish there was something I could do." I knew she was sincere.

"Thanks, Sondra. And thanks for putting up with my crap for a little while."

"Anytime, babe."

I made my way back to the office and started feeling a little better. My stomach had settled down to a steady ache, and my legs were working much better. My head was beginning to work logically again, and I began remembering things I'd read about this situation, and talks I'd had with John about the subject.

Everyone seemed to agree that the best way to handle a fear was to go through it, because anything else was simply reinforcing the fear. So how did that apply in my case? I assumed the logical thing to do would be to go back to the party and watch Pamela having sex with Ron. I'd heard people talk about that experience, and many said it was really worth it. So maybe in my self-pity I was missing a chance to make a real breakthrough.

I put on my bathrobe and headed for the party. As I got closer, I could hear the music and some voices, but they'd gotten quieter since I'd left. That made me think – what time was it? It must be close to midnight or even later. Where had the night gone?

I went to the front door, avoiding the more direct route downstairs, and entered the living room. Most of the lights had been dimmed or turned off, but I could still see three or four people in the room, and all of them were either asleep or well on their way. I turned and went through the dining room into the kitchen, noting the dishes hadn't been done, and started down the stairs.

As I entered the room, the first thing I saw was Ron and Pamela lying on a mattress opposite the staircase. But they weren't "doing" anything. They were just lying next to one another talking. The most physical contact I saw was touching each other casually.

I walked the length of the room and stopped at the bar. I poured myself a glass of ginger ale, and looked back up the room to where they were lying, but there was no change. I'm not even sure they saw me walk past.

I finished my drink and exited through the glass door. My step was lively and my legs worked just fine as I returned to the office. This time I could focus on the drawing, and I made a few changes, then something caught my eye. It was a short note penciled on the side of my drawing board. "Tom. Hope everything works out. Sorry I missed you." It was signed M. I assumed Melinda stopped b y while I was over at Sondra's. In a way, I was sorry I missed her – maybe it would have changed the whole night. But that's just another fantasy, and I'd had enough of those for one night.

The radio announced that it was five after two in the morning, and that news triggered a heavy feeling of sleepiness. I put down the pencil and climbed into bed. I had a little trouble turning off the fantasies, but I finally fell asleep.

was awakened by the sound of the door opening, and when I looked over, there stood Pamela. She showed all the signs of a long night of drinking, and her usually beautiful hair was a tangled mess. I could see daylight coming in through the door, so I guess the time had to be around 6 o'clock. I sat up in bed and greeted her. "Hi."

"Hi. Did I hurt you?"

I looked at her a long minute before replying, "Yes."

The Family

There was a very big difference between coming to Sandstone and actually living there; a whole new world of politics and intrigue you had to be part of to understand. For example, there was the "Monday Night Meeting."

The club was closed on Mondays, and most of us spent the day cleaning the house and grounds after entertaining a hundred to two hundred or more people over the weekend. The place was usually a hell of a mess. If there was one quality our members lacked, it was a feeling of responsibility for Sandstone. They seemed to look at it as a place to "do their thing" and leave. We were the "family" and they were the "members" and never should the twain meet. I admit that this feeling was shared by most of the family, and not without cause. After cleaning up the mess for a few weeks, having things stolen from the property, and constantly being made to feel we were their servants, it was difficult for the family to feel very positive about the weekend invasions.

Conducting an interview with a prospective member on a Sunday afternoon was a frightening experience, because we never knew what shape the downstairs was going to be in when we took them on a tour of the Ranch.

There were some members, a definite minority, who did have a sense of responsibility, and did help us clean up to some degree. But this was usually accomplished by a family member laying a guilt-trip on them about cleaning up their mess in the kitchen after they'd cooked. Anyway, that's how most of us spent Monday.

Monday night the family had a meeting to work out any problems we might be having, to take care of business such as the monthly newsletter, and to elicit any resentments we might have toward anyone else in the family.

Working out those resentments was a two-step process: The first step was for the two people involved to try and work it out between themselves with open, honest communication. If that didn't work, the next step was to bring it up at the meeting in front of the whole family. This could occasionally cause anxiety for some of us when we were aware that it was going to be brought up that night. More often than not, the anxiety was useless because either the topic wasn't brought up, or it would prove to be a small misunderstanding.

Anyone in the family also had the right to call a special meeting if they felt something was too important to wait for Monday night.

The meeting could be anything from a five-minute happy time to a five-hour heavy encounter. It just depended on what happened that week. Sometimes, a person would be bothered by something another family did, but would project their anger and frustration on someone completely different at the meeting. One of us, usually John, could see through that, and get the person to confront the real problem.

I used to laugh inside when a member would express an interest in attending one of our meetings (which was rare) to discuss some issue about the way we were running the club. It could also be something they had against a specific family member. What they didn't understand was that the meetings were a two-way street; if they did come to express their dissatisfaction, they had to be ready to get some feedback, not just from the person they were talking to but the whole family. Also, members weren't aware that if they expressed something to one of us, it usually did get reported at the meeting. So they did get heard.

One of the big things I noticed was a change in my attitude about the security factor of living at Sandstone. I mean security in the sense of Maslow's Needs Hierarchy. Security Needs are just above Survival. It's a little hard to describe, but I became very aware of the fact that John and Barbara Williamson "owned" Sandstone – the whole Ranch. It was theirs, and the rest of us felt that. It wasn't anything they did or said, although Barbara would occasionally make a little dig to remind us, it was more a matter of attitude. We always knew they had the option to tell us to leave. They'd done it before and they could do it again. If anyone even hinted that they were thinking of leaving, the best thing to do was to start packing. You were either committed or not. Or, as Ken Kesey used to say, "You're either on the bus or you're off."

At one point, Marty was seeing a girl named Sue he'd met at the Retreat. He went down the hill and took her to dinner and the show, and even brought her up to the Retreat for the evening. There was a lot of pressure to either have Sue move in with him or stop seeing her. The major source of the pressure was Barbara. Part of it I could understand; the time Marty spent away from the Ranch had an effect on his behavior and his value system.

Sue finally agreed to move in with him. It was a very big step for her, being a nice, pretty Jewish girl. She was afraid of what her parents would think about it – they weren't in favor of it. But she weathered the initial indignation, and they finally accepted the fact that she was doing what she really wanted to do.

Barbara and Sue started a love affair almost at once. I'm not sure how much of it was 'love' on Sue's part, and how much of it was her acceptance problem – the same one we all faced, and each of us handled it differently.

I remember talking to Sue after she and Marty returned from a trip to New York. They attended a couple of very wild swinging parties while they were there. "So how was the trip, Sue?"

"Oh, it was okay."

"Is that all?"

"Well, it was interesting," she replied.

"Did you learn anything back there in the Big Apple?"

"Yeah, I learned how to fuck without feeling." I guess she felt it was expected of her. I call it Duty Sex.

The 'love affair' had a negative effect on the Community on a couple of different levels. Marty was having trouble handling the whole thing, because he and Sue hadn't been together long enough to really form a solid relationship. There has to be a period at the beginning of a relationship when the two people should be completely monogamous. The length of time this lasts depends on the two people, and how quickly they develop strong levels of trust and respect. If either of them venture outside the relationship before those levels are established, it can be very destructive to the pair bond. Also, Marty was having trouble handling a female as competition, especially one as strong-willed as Barbara.

At a Monday night meeting, I asked Barbara if it was necessary for the two of them to be together all the time. There were things Sue could be doing if she wasn't with Barbara so much. But Barbara rejected my objections completely.

She felt the two of them needed that much time together. Since we already had the same situation with two other members of the family, Michael and Janice, our work force was definitely depleted.

Michael and Janice's situation was different in that they weren't trying to "form" a relationship. But Michael was a very possessive man who wanted nothing whatsoever to threaten their relationship. So he insured that by not letting Janice out of his sight. No matter what he was doing, she was nearby. Both of them might go nude on a warm, sunny day, but they both put their pants on when it was party time, and they rarely attended the parties.

Michael was a soft, gentle person who loved to work with flowers and plants and animals, but when it came to humans, he could have a destructive streak in him. He did beautiful things with the landscaping at the Ranch, but then he would turn around and treat Janice very cruelly. John finally had to talk to him after Janice complained that she just couldn't handle it anymore. Michael responded to the talk by bringing another woman, Tanya, up to the Ranch, moving her into the West House with Janice.

Janice must have loved Michael very much, and really wanted the relationship to work, but the addition of Tanya to the family was just too much for her. We all felt that something would have to be done to change the situation.

One afternoon Tanya and I were talking, she had a lovely British accent, and she was excited to find out I was a writer, because she'd been trying to do some writing but was having trouble getting started; the writer's dilemma of staring at a blank page in the typewriter. I agreed to show her a few of the stories I was working on, and we walked over to the cottage – where I had moved after Michael and Janice had left.

We had been sitting and talking about fifteen minutes when I heard footsteps coming down the path – I knew who it was just by the sound. There was a knock on the door and I said, "Come in." Sure enough, Michael opened the door to see me sitting in a chair with pages of text on my lap and Tanya on the bed (I only had one chair in the small space) a few feet away with some newsletters on her lap.

"Oh, sorry," was all he said. Then he closed the door and left.

"Wow, I'm going to hear about this," Tanya told me.

"Why? What's wrong with us talking?"

"You don't know Michael, he's very jealous." She handed me the newsletters and abruptly left.

I ran into Tanya the next day in the kitchen. "Everything okay?"

"Yeah, we had a bit of a hassle, but it's okay now."

Two weeks later, at a Monday night meeting, Michael informed us that he and Tanya were leaving. "I'd like to know how the rest of you feel about it," he said. There were a few minutes of silence. "Come on, I really want to know."

Marty broke the silence. "What difference would it make, Michael? You aren't going to believe us, and we're sure as hell not going to try to talk you out of leaving."

"No, I'll believe you. Really."

Barbara told him, "I think you're a coward."

Michael bristled. "What do you mean by that?"

"I mean I think you're running away from yourself."

He sneered. "Oh, come on, Barbara, that's bullshit."

"See what we mean, Michael? You won't believe us – you can't." Barbara was speaking for all of us. We didn't need to add anything.

"Well, I just want you all to know that we love you very much, and we want to feel that we can come back up any time and still be welcomed." Michael seemed to be pleading.

John answered him. "It doesn't work that way, Michael. You're going to be changing your value system out of necessity, and we're going to be changing ours, but in different directions. The two will get further apart. You can come back here, but don't expect to be greeted with open arms. And remember, this is your decision."

So Michael and Tanya left the next day, taking with them a lot of things they didn't really have any right to take. That was an example of how their value system had already started changing. They did come back up a few times, but they were just a lovely hippie couple visiting the Retreat, and they never attended a party.

Other than Monday, the rest of the week was spent doing a number of things, and sometimes doing nothing but relaxing – and thinking. Since the club was our only source of income, a lot of energy went into it. For instance, someone had to be in the living room to answer the phone. That was our main source of communication as far as memberships were concerned. It was a dull, boring job, but someone had to do it. The women probably hated it more than the men, because when they got a call from a male prospect, they had to put up with all kinds of bullshit. The callers would do everything they could to embarrass the

69

women, which was almost impossible over the phone. If the caller got too gross, the woman would end the call with "Fuck off, creep!"

There was a certain amount of required work that had to be done every day, but it usually only took two or three hours. This left all of us with plenty of time to do other things. The things that had to be done included answering the phone, interviewing prospective members when they showed up, writing and publishing a monthly newsletter, planning special events like the annual Valentines Day party (by invitation only), and when time allowed, planning other activities for the Foundation besides club-related ones. The workload was accomplished on two levels: One was the level of what had to be done, which included doing the dishes, mowing and watering the lawn, cleaning leaves off the driveway, etc. The other level was teleocratic – based on a person's abilities. Since John's background was engineering, he handled the machinery maintenance. He was also the only one who knew how to drive a tractor, so he did that.

My background was writing and graphics, so I published the monthly newsletter and any other literature we might generate. I also assumed management of the club. That involved registering members and guests when they arrived, and collecting any fees. Also, keeping an eye on things downstairs to make sure everyone was happy.

Marty was managing the club when I moved to Sandstone, but when he and Sue started their relationship, they needed time together, so I inherited the job. It seems that the club has been managed by single males for most of its existence. When I took over the job, Marty started handling public relations, and that remained his role for the rest of the time the Retreat was open.

Barbara's specialty was the finances. She was the only one who had a system worked out. Everyone was responsible for getting receipts for purchases, and keeping the desk log up-to-date and accurate, but Barbara handled the overall bookkeeping chores. She was also very good at interviewing – she didn't take shit from any one; here's what it is, this is how much it costs, take it or leave it.

 Sue's main task was taking care of the club's membership records, typing the monthly billings, and helping Marty with public relations.

Janice spent most of her time outdoors working on the plants and flowers, keeping them watered – which was a big job in the hot, dry summers. There were times when all of us took a few hours and converged on the hoses.

70

During the early part of 1972 the family went through some big changes. Tutt and Marcia had already left, and even before Michael and Tanya left, we lost one of the stronger members of the family.

I came home from the city one Monday and walked into the living room where John, Barbara and Marty were sitting. The trip down the hill hadn't been too successful – dealing with printers never is.

The minute I saw them, I knew something was wrong, and asked what it was.

"Sondra's leaving."

"What? You're kidding. I mean, what's she doing, going on a vacation or something?"

"Nope, she's moving out."

"Well, where is she right now?" I asked.

"Up at the West House packing."

I hurried up to the West House completely confused. Sondra was our tower of strength! What could have happened? We knew she was acting a little strange lately, but for a psychic person like her, that wasn't too unusual.

When I walked in the West House, she was leaning over the bed with her back to me. I spoke her name and she turned around. I couldn't believe it! This wasn't the face of Sondra. This was some totally psychotic, wild-eyed person inhabiting her body.

"Sondra?"

"Oh, Tom. I'm so glad you're here." Her voice was shaky, almost panicky.

"What's going on?" I asked.

"Tom, you've got to get out of here. Come with me. I'll take you down the hill, anyplace you want. Just come with me."

"Why, sweetheart? What's the matter?"

"Christ, Tom! Don't you know what they're doing up here?"

"I'm not sure. Why don't you tell me."

"This is a laboratory, Tom. Don't you see that? They're experimenting with our minds to see how much emotional pain we can stand!"

Zap! Raging paranoia.

I turned around and started to leave, her voice getting harder to hear. "Go pack, Tom, and I'll meet you at the car. Hurry!"

We didn't have a Monday night meeting that week; none of us felt up to it. I saw Sondra once more as she was driving out, and she stopped long enough to reiterate her warning to me. I told her I was sorry, but I had to stay, just to find out for myself.

Doug joined the community shortly after Sondra's departure. I must admit, I had some reservations about Doug moving in, but it was never brought up at a meeting, and I never expressed my feelings to the few people who asked about it. It wasn't really fair of me to pre-judge that radically, but all I saw was another single male moving in who didn't seem very committed to anything. Obviously John and Barbara invited him, so we didn't really have any say-so in the matter.

Little did I know that he was a gourmet chef at the young age of 21, and one of the hardest workers in the community (except he refused to clean the kitchen after he'd made a mess). He cooked us some fantastic meals, and that wasn't easy on our continually short budget.

Shortly after he moved in, he and Janice tried to get a relationship going, but it was doomed to fail almost from the start. Janice had a far-out fantasy about the man she was going to love, and Doug didn't come close. Also, she was still pretty shaken by Michael and Tanya's departure, and that could have had something to do with it.

Butch and Sheri left shortly after that, but for entirely different reasons than Sondra. They had trouble handling the whole concept of "Community". They finally decided it just wasn't their lifestyle, especially Butch. He put possession of money very high on his priority list, and Community contradicted that idea. He was a mechanic, and when his head was on straight, a damn good one. But he expected to get paid for working on cars that belonged to other members of the family, and we didn't feel he was justified in charging us. So it was mutually agreed that they move out.

So the family had finally settled down to eight of us; John and Barbara, Marty and Sue, Doug, Janice and her daughter, and myself.

I feel the critical factor in having a synergistic "Inner Community" lay in the selection process – which was entirely up to the Williamsons, and I never did find out what criteria they used. There was never any "consensus" vote by the rest of us living there. I didn't know from one day to the next who would be living at the Ranch. Obviously, Gay Talese was there to write about us, and Jon and Bunny Dana were there to produce a movie. Was the movie a result of synergy? Definitely not. Maybe during the filming, but during the critical editing process, the three of them, Jon and Bunny and Pat Darrin fought constantly –

they each had their own view of what the finished product should be, and the movie that was eventually released was a reflection of those differences.

But where did the other temporary residents come from and how were they selected? What purpose did they serve? At times, there as many as twelve living at the Ranch. I was there because of my writing and graphic skills, and I eventually took over as manager of the Retreat, but during my time at Sandstone, I saw very little involvement by all the others with the operation of the private club – which was our only source of income. Granted, some of them did put an effort into maintaining the physical environment, important functions to be sure and we all pitched in, but where were they during the Wednesday night potlucks and the Saturday night parties interacting with the members, explaining our philosophy – if they knew it?

I had a few arguments with Barbara Williamson at our Monday night meetings about the way she gave permission for single men, like Gay Talese and Bob Francoeur, to attend the Saturday night parties if she felt they could benefit Sandstone, and the feedback I received from members. But the fact that my continued residence was determined by them was always lurking at the back of my mind, so I never pushed too hard.

The Massaging Ball-Buster

It was a Wednesday night; we'd had a delicious pot-luck with corned beef for an entrée and what seemed like dozens of side dishes. I'd gone downstairs to see what the party was like, and everyone seemed to be having fun. The atmosphere was very warm and inviting with soft music coming from the stereo.

I was standing nude at the opposite end of the long room, leaning against a padded massage table. One wall of the room was divided by a large stone fireplace, just as there was one upstairs in the living room. The glowing coals were putting out a minimum of heat and a small pool of orange light directly in front of it. The only other light was provided by a number of small fixtures in the ceiling that only accentuated the deep pile, blood-red carpeting.

73

It was a very surreal scene for me. Taking in the whole scene at once was almost impossible, because the mattresses and part of the carpet were covered with about 60 people who seemed to be in a constant state of motion – all either partly dressed or nude. Maybe one or two women wearing panties (this was a more conservative group that our Saturday night party-goers, or maybe they were in their period), a couple of guys wearing shirts for some odd reason. It was almost too much visual input to take in all at once. Every time I'd try to sweep the room, my eyes would get stuck on a lovely female body or a couple in an embrace. So many people! So much bare flesh! This was my environment.

Suddenly, I was aware of someone standing beside me. I turned my head enough to see a very lovely female profile. She was also nude, about five-four, long black hair that fell down over her shoulders almost touching the erect nipples on nicely shaped breasts. As my gaze continued down over her flat belly to the puff of black hair, I became aware that she was looking at me. I quickly, almost guiltily, brought my eyes back up to her face. She was smiling slightly, with an edge of nervousness showing at the corners of her full lips.

"Are you next in line for a massage?" she asked, her voice also betraying the nervousness.

"Yeah, I guess so. Where's Paul?"

"He went upstairs to get something to drink. He'll be right back. Why don't you get up on the table?" She put her hand on the table beside me.

"Okay," I said as I started to lie down on the cool leather. "Are you his assistant?"

"Well, actually, I'm a student. I work as a therapist, and Paul is teaching me how to incorporate massage into my therapy. You're going to be my first patient."

"You mean you're going to give me a massage?" I was lying on my stomach.

"Yes."

"Wonderful. I'm Tom"

"I'm Terri."

"With an i?"

She smiled, "Yes."

She positioned a folded towel under my head and her hands felt good, though I could feel a slight quiver. I'm excited and she's nervous.

I turned my head sideways to look at the room – it looked even stranger from that perspective. I couldn't discern individuals, just a lot of beautiful naked flesh

74

in all kinds of positions. I turned my head back straight and lifted it off the towel. I could make out a few individuals I knew. Then I laid my head back down and let all those bodies float together in a blur.

I was enjoying the kaleidoscopic view of the bodies when I felt a slight breeze as someone moved next to me.

"Well, is this our next victim?" It was Paul. I'd met him before, and enjoyed our conversations. I didn't know he gave massages.

"Hi, Paul. You going to give me a workout?"

"Well, not exactly. This will be more of a sensual massage than a muscular rubdown." I felt his big hand on my shoulder.

"That sounds even better. I think I'm ready for just about anything." At that point, I had no idea what "anything" was, but I was ready to find out.

"First of all," Paul told me, "I want you to put your head straight down and rest your forehead on the towel." I did as he instructed.

"Now. Are you completely comfortable?"

I checked myself out, and found that my neck was a little stiff in that position but not really uncomfortable. Then I realized I was laying on my penis, and that was definitely uncomfortable. So I lifted up a little and moved it down between my legs. Then I felt pressure on my toes, so I changed the position of my feet. "Okay, Paul, I feel very comfortable." I really did. The leather cover on the table had warmed up to my body temperature, and I could feel my whole body letting go. I think it would have felt good to just laying there like that for a while.

"Next, we have the oil." I figured out he was talking to Terri, not me. "I use this oil. It's almond and feels and smells very good." I immediately became aware of the new aroma around my head. He was right – it did smell good. "First, you put some in the palms of your hands, then rub your hands together a minute. That gets the oil up to body temperature, so it will feel comfortable when you apply it to his skin."

Although my head was in a position that kept me from seeing what was happening, my other senses were working just fine, because I could hear him rubbing his hands together.

"Now watch how I make the initial contact with his skin." I could tell from his voice that Paul was standing right in front of my head. As he leaned over me, I felt the pressure of his body move the table slightly, I could sense the increase in warmth emanating from him, and it seemed as though his hands were floating just above my shoulders.

His first contact was soft and gentle, just barely touching my shoulders. Then, as his hands began moving down my back and spread apart, he increased the pressure. By the time he reached the small of my back and began moving back up, he was pressing me down on the table. His hands came back up to the outside edges of my back, and I had the strangest sensation of possessing eyes that could 'see' wherever his hands touched.

He continued working on my back for a few minutes, then stopped. I was almost sorry, because the more he did it the better it felt.

"I'm going to work on his legs now. You continue working on his back, doing just what I was doing." As he spoke, I felt his voice move away from my head and changing in volume as he went to the other end of the table. I could only assume (and hope!) he was talking to Terri.

Well now, this was going to be interesting. I'd never been massaged by a female when we were both nude. Especially when there was going to be a male working on me at the same time.

"Remember what I told you about the oil." He was starting to touch my calves now, working down to my feet.

Suddenly, I felt another pair of hands on my shoulders. Much cooler hands, smaller, more tentative. Nervous fingers seems to be exploring my back instead of really touching it.

"No, no. not like that. Here, let me show you." His voice returned to the previous location above my head. I felt his hands on top of hers, guiding her in the stroke and putting more pressure on them. "That's right. Now just keep that up." His voice was moving back down to my feet.

I decided to focus on what Terri was doing. Her hands, still unsure, moved slowly down my back. I felt her weight leaning against the table as she stretched over me; then the most sensational realization of her nipples brushing my shoulders again. What a sensation!

Another sensation I became aware of at about the same time was the beginnings of an erection. Well, that's to be expected, I guess. Not much I can do about it.

My neck was beginning to ache, so I decided to move it for a minute. I lifted my head, rested my chin on the towel and there, just inches away was her lovely pubis! What a beautiful sight! I couldn't remember if I'd ever taken the time to just look at it close up before my lips made contact. Every lush, dark, curly hair stood out in detail, and the crease between her labia was barely visible above the edge of the table.

Now there was no doubt about my erection, it was pushing uncomfortably against the table. I also felt Paul's hands on the backs of my knees, and working up my thighs. His hands were firmly exploring my muscles – clear up to and including my ass. What if he touches my genitals? How am I going to react to that?

No sooner did I ask the question than it was answered – his hand did brush my genitals. Then his other hand did the same. It didn't seem to bother him. I was getting much too involved in the sensual pleasure of four hands moving over my body to even care anymore. That realization surprised me since I had many of the same homophobic fears most men have. Suddenly, there was nothing to fear and everything to enjoy.

Paul moved back down to my feet, and Terri had moved to one side of the table and was massaging my arm and hand. Then she shifted her attention to my lower back and ass. Four hands moving over my body, and I gave up trying to keep track of them. Suddenly, the touch got much softer, then stopped altogether.

Paul told me, "Okay, turn over and we'll do the other side."

At first, I couldn't get my body to work right, but with a great deal of effort, and a little help from the two of them, I was able to turn over on my back.

In this new position, the sensations were very different. I was aware of a cool breeze moving over my stomach that I assumed was caused by the movement of my two massagers moving around the table, and the fact that my body had been warmed by the leather cover on the table. Of course, the massage itself had something to do with it also, since I'm sure my blood was moving faster – at least in certain parts of my body; I became even more aware of my semi-erection. This was momentarily embarrassing, but since I'd been in this situation before, the embarrassment didn't last long.

The first time that had happened, I'd been upstairs just talking to a young woman and we both got very turned on to each other. She almost led me downstairs by my penis! While those things were going through my mind, Paul was talking to Terri. "Now, let's get some oil on our hands before we begin." Since they were standing at the head of the table, I couldn't see them too well without stretching my neck, so I just relaxed and let them talk.

Terri asked, "Do you want me to work on his legs this time?"

"No," Paul replied, "I want you to continue working on his upper torso until you get that series of strokes down perfect."

"Okay," she replied. "Do I use the same stroke as I did on his back?"

"Yes, hands together going down the middle, then spread them when you come back up; all in a slow, circular motion. Here, let me show you." I could feel Paul's hands hovering over my chest.

Once again he began with a very light stroke, but it got stronger as he moved down my chest to my stomach. When his hands touch my pubic hair, he spread them apart and brought them back up to my shoulders. It was easy to tell that he knew what he was doing; the touch, the stroke, everything was very confident. Just the right speed and pressure, definitely not the normal kneading and twisting massage.

Then Paul moved down to the foot of the table and began working on my left leg. It felt good, but I must admit I was much more interested in what Terri was getting ready to do.

I felt the pressure of her body leaning against the table above my head, and could almost tell what she was doing without seeing her. I saw the shadow of her hands pass in front of my face, and very gently, tentatively, her hands touch my chest and began their brief journey down the middle with her thumbs together. The pressure increased slightly as she reached my stomach, but at the first touch of my pubic hair, her hands quickly parted and began coming back up my sides. She repeated that process three or four times before I noticed a distinct difference in her touch. For one thing, her fingers weren't jerking away when they touched my pubic hair, and she was leaning her whole body over my face when her hands were moving down to my stomach.

On about the seventh pass she was making, I felt the strangest sensation of her nipples touching my temples! At the farthest point of her stretch, her fingers touched the base of my penis before she spread her hands and began coming back up. This was more like it! She was finally getting into the sensual part.

All the while Terri was caressing my upper torso, I'd lost interest in what Paul was doing. In fact, he'd moved up to my thighs, and when his fingers reached the top of the stroke, they came into contact with Terri's. I hardly think that was an accident, because they made a point of doing it again. All this time Terri's erect nipples were touching my skin continuously because she neglected to straighten up when her hands were back up on my chest. She moved her hands, not her body. My erection was no longer "semi".

78

During the time the two of them were massaging me, there were 50 or 60 people in the room. Along with all the other sensual input I was receiving, I was at least partly aware of the sounds around me. The music, the soft conversations highlighted by bursts of laughter and louder screams of pleasure became part of the whole experience – the gestalt.

Terri was doing very nice things on my face with her fingertips. I leaned my head back and there were her breasts with hard nipples. I wasn't the only one with an erection. I reached up and cupped her breasts in my hands, resting one finger on her nipples.

She looked down at me and smiled, "I thought we were the ones doing the massage."

"Do you mind?"

"No, not at all. I think we're about finished."

Just then I heard a female voice call my name, and turned my head to see who it was. Actually there were three females and they were all headed for the massage table. One of said, "Hey, that looks like fun. Can we help?"

"Sure, join in," Paul told them with a laugh. "Terri, give them the oil." The three newcomers spread themselves around me. Suddenly, I was surrounded by beautiful naked bodies! There were ten hands touching me at the same time, and I could feel differences in all of them. At first, I tried to keep track of whose hands were doing what to me and where, but it quickly got to be too much effort. I just relaxed and let them move.

Surprisingly, I flashed back to my childhood. My parents were never physically affectionate (does an enema count?), so I looked for it in my peer group. Granted, most of the boys used aggression and sports to give themselves permission to touch, but I was raised at the beach where we rarely wore more than a brief swimsuit – and that got partially removed when we unselfconsciously washed the sand out after a volleyball game. So we touched more, boys with boys, but mostly boys with girls and girls with each other. We were definitely not body-shy – at the beach. Remembering those times was fun, but I switched it off when I felt something new.

One of the strangest sensations occurred when one of them leaned her head down and started swishing her long, soft hair across my stomach. It almost tickled, but not quite. This "massage" was definitely changing its mood fast. Two of the women were much more interested in my very erect cock than the rest of my body. Terri was still working on my face, but her fingers indicated she was

79

not pleased with the intrusion of the other three. The pressure was a little harder, and her fingers were moving faster. Her attention was obviously split. Paul was still working on my feet, but his touch had also changed. I glanced down toward my feet and discovered that one girl was keeping one hand on me, but the other hand was caressing Paul's chest and stomach. That explained the change in his business-like attitude that I'd felt up to now.

Suddenly, I was aware that the one who had been swishing her hair across my stomach had move d her head down and was now rubbing her face against my cock. That caused me to lose track of what all the others were doing. Then she took it into her mouth. I'm sure the other hands were still moving over my body, but that was on a secondary level. My primary sensory input was from the woman who was now giving me head. And was she giving! Her hands were busy caressing my testicles and thighs while her mouth was busy on my cock. All this time, her face was completely hidden by that mass of soft black hair that kept moving, but not exposing, every time she changed position even slightly.

After a very few minutes of all that attention, I had a tremendous orgasm that engulfed my whole body. There were squeals and yelps of laughter as I jerked convulsively until I almost rolled off the table. The whole gang had to hold me down.

Then I did relax – completely. I felt wrung-out. Everyone gave me a few final touches, then moved away. I looked up long enough to smile weakly but gratefully at the lady who had been the instrument of that tremendous orgasm. She smiled back knowingly. The only one who didn't leave was Terri. Even Paul was walking toward a mattress with his arm about the lady who had been caressing him a few minutes earlier.

I felt her hands resting on my shoulders while I lay there trying to regain enough strength to move. Finally, with great effort, I sat up, turned and swung my legs over the side. I turned my head sideways to see Terri looking at me.

I said, "I could use a cup of coffee. You want to come upstairs with me?" I held out my hand and she took it without saying a word.

When we reached the stairway, I moved aside and let her lead the way. This wasn't so much chivalry as it was selfish; with her two steps ahead of me, my eyes were right in line with her lovely butt, and that was an enjoyable view as she moved from step to step. So enjoyable in fact that halfway up I leaned forward and kissed one cheek. She looked back over her shoulder and smiled.

I stopped in the kitchen, which was still a mess from the sumptuous meal we'd had earlier, and got my cup of coffee. Terri declined. Then I followed Terri through the dining room into the large living room with its deep gold, shag carpeting and rich furniture. The whole room was dimly lit by small fixtures hidden on the rough-hewn beams. The house had been built back in 1934, but the original group that moved there from the Valley had done an amazing renovation.

We mutually agreed to sit on one of the couches that was positioned away from the center conversation area. It had two heavy mahogany end tables in front of it that were littered with empty plastic cups and glasses…more remnants from the dinner, which I gathered up and took to the large fireplace that reigned over the whole room. As I walked back to the couch where Terri was sitting, I took a long look at her. I was beginning to feel very good about her. She was sitting on the couch with her legs curled up under her, looking around the room almost as if she'd never seen it before. That gave me the opportunity to study her. She was a very lovely young woman with a well-proportioned body topped by a pretty face surrounded by long, wavy black hair. I tried to read her body language, but they were confusing. Her posture was defensive, but she had a way of looking at me with a small, sweet smile that changed to a downward glance in a few seconds.

As I sat down beside her, she asked, "You're kind of the manager here, aren't you, Tom?"

"Kinda," I replied vaguely. I was also "kinda" playing with her, hoping to draw her out a little.

"Why?"

That one caught me off guard. "Why what?"

"Why are you here? What are you looking for?"

I laughed softly, "Is this therapy?"

"No, I'm just curious." There was that downward glance again.

"Well, do you want the standard tape-recorded simplistic answer, or shall we delve into a deep philosophical discussion?"

When she looked at me, she saw the facetious smile, and knew I was playing with her. "Forget it."

"I'm sorry, Terri. It's just that I get asked that question a lot, and usually just to maintain contact. The people asking aren't even interested in the answer. Besides, that was a pretty broad question. Couldn't we start with something easier?" As I spoke, I reached over and put my hand gently on her arm. Her skin felt cool and soft.

"Please don't do that." It was more a soft pleading than a demand.

I slowly ran my hand down the full length of her arm and hand then returned it to my side of the couch. I saw a slight shiver go through her as I did it. We sat silently for a couple of minutes. Since she wouldn't look at me, I once again took a closer look at her. Now she was in profile. Her face was more Eastern from that angle, more Arabic than Jewish. Her breasts weren't large, but they were perfectly formed and the nipples were still very erect. Her stomach was flat, even in the sitting position.

"Well?"

Once again she caught me off guard. "Well what?"

"Do you like what you see?" Her voice was slightly petulant.

"Very much, Terri. I think you're a very beautiful girl."

"Do you want to make love to me?"

She was full of surprises. "The thought has crossed my mind."

"Do you live here all the time?" She seemed to have ignored my answer.

"Yes." I decided to play along with her a little while longer.

"Do you work in the city, or ever go down there for any reason?"

"No, I don't work in the city, and yes, I do go down there when it's necessary."

"I don't blame you," she replied. "If I lived on top of this mountain, it would take an emergency to get me down there." She sounded a bit sad.

I laughed softly. "Well, sometimes all it takes is hunger. We have to buy our groceries down the hill."

"Oh, yeah." She paused a few seconds then asked the obvious question. "What is this place? Is it just a fuck club?"

I put my hand on her knee. "For some people, that's all it is. What have you got against sex?"

"Nothing, really." She was looking down.

"Look, Terri, Sandstone is different for every person who comes here. Yes, for some it is a fuck club, but that's because they have the freedom here to work through their sexual fantasies – as long as they aren't too kinky. For others it's a lot more. I can't tell you what it is except what it is for me."

"What is it for you?"

Well, I'd asked her upstairs to talk, so I guess that's what we're going to do – for now. "Basically, the Retreat provides a consensus. The people who live here and visit share many of my values and lifestyle choices. It's a place to work on relationships, and to find out how you feel about yourself and your partner, especially with regard to sexuality. People come here and they can do almost anything they want to do, but they don't have to do anything. It's completely up to the individual. It's what we call a permission-giving environment. Each person has to give themselves permission. That's not easy."

"Boy, I'll go along with that!" she said through pouted lips. "But you don't have a relationship here. Do you?"

"No, not right now. But I plan to have a Primary Relationship within this lifestyle. That means with complete openness and honesty and permission-giving."

"That's not easy. What about jealousy?"

"Well, you're a therapist. How do you handle jealousy with your patients?"

"Oh, come on, Tom. Working in a mental hospital isn't quite the same as this. Mainly, we just talk about it if it comes up, which isn't often."

"Okay, we talk about it too. The difference is we have some change mechanisms here you don't have in that mental hospital – although they would help."

"Like what?" Now she seemed genuinely interested, and her body language changed; she was looking at me, her legs were out from under her, more "open."

"Casual nudity is one change mechanism. Nude people are much more aware of themselves physically. It also changes the level of communication between people. For instance, I'm getting a lot of non-verbal communication from you right now, and it's changed; the way you sit and look at me instead of your navel. Maybe you should try it at that hospital."

"Ha! Are you kidding?" She laughed at the idea. "I would no more be in the same room with nuts nude than…well, I just wouldn't."

"That's too bad, Terri. It's been known to facilitate therapy. Naked people are more honest."

"Yeah, it could also facilitate me getting raped, too!"

"Well, I doubt that. But it would definitely open up communication." I was trying to concentrate on the conversation, but her body language was turning me on. "Anyway, Terri, another change mechanism here is the open sexuality." Her expression, her whole body 'cooled' at the mention of sexuality. She didn't reply, so I plunged on. "What I mean is there are three reasons why people should have sex in the open."

"What are they?" she asked softly.

"First, if the sex thing is 'blocking' the relationship. Two people want to get know each other, but one or both of is so turned on they can't think of much else. It's best to just go ahead and do it, get it out of the way. Then you can learn more about each other. Although the second reason is that you'll never 'know' a person fully without having sex with them. So maybe having sex will tell you whether you really want to pursue the relationship. The third reason is very simple – it's fun and it feels good."

She'd been sitting very still during my short lecture, keeping her eyes down, her lips pouted. "And that, lovely Terri, is where we're at right now." I put my hand on the back of her neck and rubbed gently.

"What do you mean?" She already knew the answer.

"You know what I mean. Sex is blocking our relationship. I'm having trouble holding this intellectual conversation when what I really want to do is take you back downstairs and make long, slow love to you." While I spoke, I moved my hand from her back to her shoulder, then down to her breast, The nipple seemed to get even harder under my fingers.

Without seeming to even be aware of what I was doing, Terri turned and said, "You're nice, Tom, so I'll give you some advice; go away and leave me alone or I'll castrate you." She said it so calmly, it took a moment for me to understand what she'd said.

"What?"

"I mean it. I could really like you, but before I let myself, I'd castrate you first – not physically, of course." She was so matter-of-fact about it.

"Why, Terri? What have you got against me?"

"Nothing, really. That's just the way I am. Oh, and I'm very good at it." This last was almost a challenge.

I took my hand away and just look at her. "Well, Terri, you may be 'pretty good,' but I've met ball-busters before, and I assure you, you're not 'very good' at it." I felt myself getting a little angry. "I've been trying to figure out why I've been getting all the mixed signals tonight, and now I know. But if you were 'really good' as you say, I'd be sitting here with a hard-on and you'd be acting differently."

84

"Like I said, Tom, I could like you – very much. That's why I'm not trying real hard. But I could if I wanted to." This sounded like a little girl trying to convince me of something she wasn't sure of.

I got serious. "I don't think it would be constructive for either of us to find out. Terri, I don't know why you hate men, but there's a good party going on downstairs and I'm not going to get into it with you. Enough intellectualizing."

We looked at each other, and we were both sad. Maybe for different reasons, but we shared that sadness. First of all, I was sad to see a ball-busting psychologist; how much good could she really do trying to help couples who were having sexual problems? It was also sad to see such a lovely person wasting her energies negatively instead of letting go. But I wasn't sad enough to try and thaw her out. I took her hand in mine, kissed her fingertips, then got up and left.

I saw her a few times during the night, usually alone but sometimes talking to a man. Mostly just observing. And the signals were no longer confusing; there was a big red neon sign on her forehead saying, "DON'T EVEN TRY IT."

The Candy Store Fantasy

After my encounter upstairs, it was a pleasure to get back downstairs and join the party. I walked the length of the room, smiling and speaking to a few of the people I knew or just watching couples – or more – enjoy themselves and each other, and sat down at the bar. It was a nice place to sit because it provided a clear view of the entire room and everything going on in it – a voyeur's delight.

There was a fellow leaning against the far end of the bar that I'd promised myself I'd keep an eye on, and this gave me a good opportunity. His name was Bill, and he'd shown up just before dinner with his wife. He'd come up about 10 days earlier inquiring about membership. I'd interviewed him And gave him the tour, and after deciding he wasn't going to burn the place down or kill anybody, invited him to one of our Wednesday night pot-lucks to get a better idea of what it was all about before spending his $240.00. This was a fairly common practice among family members who did the interviewing. We rarely invited newcomers to a Saturday night party as an introduction – Saturday night parties could get slightly intense. There was a lot more sexual activity and the whole party had a more urgent feel to it.

The Wednesday night pot-lucks were more low-key. There was a greater degree of sociability than on a Saturday night, and only about half the people. The majority came up for the dinner and to interact with old friends and new members. On Saturday night the majority showed up after dinner and went straight downstairs.

Bill and his wife, I'll call her Judith, had decided to take advantage of the opportunity to attend one of our pot-lucks. I met them at the door and had them fill out guest cards. That gave me a chance to assess his wife, get a feel for how she was feeling about being here. And she wanted to be someplace else. She was upset when she looked around the living room and saw all the nude people – obviously casual nudity was not part of their lifestyle. I tentatively decided this was all Bill's idea, and Judith was his ticket to get in the front door. I'd told him we only allowed couples at the parties.

Bill rapidly took off his shirt and shoes and socks, but Judith left all her clothes on, and was even more uncomfortable when he started downstairs after dinner wearing only his pants. I tried to impress on her how everything was optional at Sandstone when I'd first met her at the door and noticed how uncomfortable she was, but I don't think she heard a word I said. And if she did, Bill was trying to over-ride my little speech, trying to coerce her into doing something she didn't want to do. But because she was his wife, rather than an individual married to him, she felt the pressure.

That had happened hours ago, and now I was watching Bill as he stood at the bar looking over the prospects. It was a classic example of what we called "The Candy Store Fantasy." He was in the candy store, and couldn't decide which flavor to try first – there was quite a selection! He probably planned on 'tasting' all of them before the night was over, but he was off to a slow start.

Two things happened almost simultaneously: A young woman came over to Bill and started talking to him, and I saw his wife come into the room with a friend of mine – she'd left her clothes upstairs. She was smiling and relaxed, as my friend led her to an empty mattress. Bill was unaware of all this; he was busy playing games with the woman who had approached him. I knew her, and I knew that she didn't want to play games, she wanted sex.

She finally convinced Bill that she wasn't interested in talking about it by taking his hand and leading him over to a mattress. Now I really perked up, because she was leading him toward the mattress where my friend and Judith were lying. He was practically on top of her before he recognized his wife, and his reaction was complete shock. That wasn't part of his fantasy. She was supposed to be upstairs reading a Magazine.

He kicked Judith's foot. "Hey! What are you doing?"

"Huh? Oh, hi, honey, this is Jerry. Jerry, this is my husband." Jerry rolled over on his back, exposing his erection. "Hi, Bill, I'm Jerry." That's all it took for Bill.

"I want to talk to you."

"Who? Me?"

"No! Her."

"Oh, right now?"

"Yes! Right now!"

"Yes, dear," she mumbled. She was still his wife, not an individual. She patted Jerry's thigh, then got up.

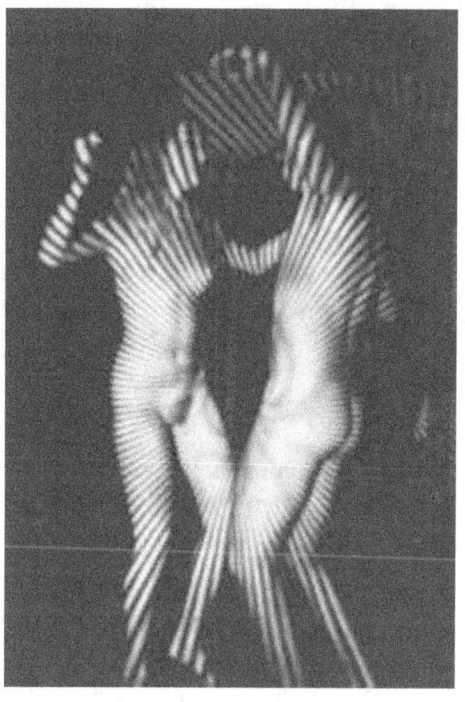

I watched all this as if I was watching a repeat performance of a play: the same scene, the same script, just different actors. As long as the 'actors' didn't get violent, we didn't interrupt. But it was a frustrating scene for all of us in the Family to watch. It was difficult to decide who you were more disappointed in, him for being a chauvinist asshole, or her for being so much less than she could be.

Bill and Judith didn't join Sandstone Retreat.

The Door

One of my main responsibilities as manager of the Retreat was working at the door, greeting people when they arrived, signing them in, checking their membership status or having them fill out guest cards, and collecting any dues or fees. I tried to make people coming for the first time aware of what it was all about even though I knew it was going to be different for each person.

Sound simple? Well, it wasn't. Nobody really liked working the door on a Saturday night, but someone had to so I accepted the job. Actually, it was one of the most interesting club functions, and provided me with a lot of fun, frustration, friends and enemies.

At least a half dozen times during my five years at Sandstone I would be surprised by a knock on the door. Most members didn't knock, they just walked in, so when someone did, it meant they'd never been at Sandstone before and didn't know what it was. On one occasion we opened the door and found ourselves face-to-face with a very nice man selling the *Watchtower*! We were nude, and I'm not sure who was more embarrassed. John invited the man in, and they had a long conversation about religion. Of course he never got around to taking his clothes off, but that's okay. He seemed to be on a very positive mission and we always enjoyed meeting such people.

You have to remember that being a member of the Retreat was not the same as belonging to the Elks or a local Country Club. Some of our members even used pseudonyms while at the Retreat, and we would occasionally get a phone call about the first of the month from a female;

"Hello, Sandstone."

"Uh…hello. Could you please tell me what kind of business this is?"

"Yes, ma'm. This is a private club. Why do you ask?"

"Well, could you tell me what your phone number is doing on our phone bill?"

"Well, sometimes children call us as a gag. We do advertise. Maybe that would explain it."

"We don't have any children."

"Oh."

"What kind of club is this?"

"Well, we call it a permission-giving environment. Our members can do just about anything they want to do while they're here, but they don't have to do anything. We have no restrictions against casual nudity, and we encourage touching and lovemaking."

"Uh-huh. Is it the type of place a man might go to meet girls?" Her voice would start to get a little more agitated by now.

"No, it's not a good place to meet girls because we require that people come to the parties as couples. Of course, after the two of you are here, there's the opportunity to meet a lot of other people, both men and women."

"I could also meet my own husband there, couldn't I?" Click. That was just one reason our members desired anonymity. Some of our members were very well known in their chosen professions, and felt their association with Sandstone might hurt them – if it was known. There was some validity to that fear as Barbara Williamson found out. She was fired from her position as a top salesperson with a large insurance company after appearing on the "Dick Cavette Show".

As a result of an incident that happened in December of 1971, we were forced to tighten our rules regarding accurate identification. You could be anyone you wanted to be at a party, but we had to have accurate records for our own protection.

John and Barbara and Marty and Sue had gone to a conference on Alternative Lifestyles one weekend, so I was sleeping in the bedroom in the main house instead of in my cottage to be more available. I was awakened Sunday morning about six-thirty by a very lovely blond woman who I knew was the guest of one of our members.

"Excuse me, Tom. Are you awake?" Her voice sounded strange.

I got out of bed and opened the door. "Yeah, sure. What's up?"

"Well, there's a girl lying downstairs in the Ballroom, and I don't think she's breathing."

"What!"

"I said there's a…"

"Sorry, I heard what you said. Hold on." I shook my head and rubbed my eyes, hoping it was a bad dream. But when I opened my eyes she was still there. "Okay, let's go see."

As we walked downstairs a million thoughts went through my head, all of them confused. I'm hardly religious, but I was praying she was wrong.

We got downstairs and I began to walk the length of the room. My escort stopped at the bar where her escort was sitting. There were three or four other couples lying on the mattresses asleep. I could barely see my escort's date at the bar, it was so dark. "Hi, George. Where is she?"

He cocked his head in the direction of the Ballroom. "She's in there, Tom, and she really looks dead."

My stomach did a flip-flop. I walked around the end of the bar, through the small bathroom, and into the Ballroom. The woman was lying face down with her arms folded under her. I could "feel" death before I even checked to see if she was breathing or had a pulse. I walked over to the mattress, knelt down and put my hand on her shoulder. Her skin felt cool, and when I started to roll her over, I could barely lift her off the mattress – and she was a thin woman. I saw her face and that was all I needed. The whole front of her nude body was discolored a strange red and blue, almost like body paint. She was definitely dead!

I walked out of the room totally shaken, knowing that certain things had to be done. There were no doors between the big room and the Ballroom, so I couldn't isolate it. I told George and his date to please go upstairs. Then I went to the other people in the room and woke them. "Please don't ask any questions, there's been some trouble. Please put some clothes on, go upstairs and wait for me." Bless their ever-lovin' hearts, they did exactly what I told them to do. Everyone eventually went upstairs.

I went back upstairs and called the police. Then I told the group what had happened, and that they would have to stay until the police arrived. I didn't bother asking if anyone knew the young woman because they hadn't seen her, but I did notice that no one came forward saying they knew her. Who was she with? I felt like this was something out of an old fifties movie, but I knew it was for real.

I think I went up to the West House and woke Michael and Janice, but I'm not sure. I was operating on automatic control. The next thing I remember is that the main house was swarming with cops. It started with one squad car, then another, then two unmarked cars from homicide followed by the coroner's station wagon.

The first question they asked stumped me. "Who is she?"

I was sitting at the bar watching the procession of uniforms and plainclothesmen going in and coming out of the ballroom. From the brief glimpse I had of her face, I had no idea who she was. I tried to picture her lying on the mattress, and all I could come up with is that she was young, had a nice body and long dark hair. Shit! We had maybe sixty people here last night. That description could fit at least a dozen women I signed in at the door – and most of them had gone home.

Suddenly, a detective appeared beside me with a purse. He was holding a driver's license. "Is this her?"

I looked at the picture and recognized a young woman I'd seen a couple of times, but had never even talked to her. I did remember that she came to last night's party. "It could be," was the best I could tell the detective. I noticed on the license that the woman was 26-years old. The officer took the license in the Ballroom, then returned in a few minutes. "That's her."

Sweet Sherri came down from the North House and was doing her best to supply the small mob with coffee. She even scrambled some eggs for us. The rest of the family were doing other things that had to be done. It was almost as if we'd rehearsed the thing and each person was playing their role. Tutt and Marcia and Michael blocked off both roads into the Ranch. Janice and Sherri were in the kitchen, and I'm not sure about the rest.

At one point a lieutenant came over to me and said, "This is really weird. I was with your brother on another homicide all night. I just left him about two hours ago. Boy, wait until he hears about this one!" My brother was a lieutenant with the sheriff's department.

Another cop started asking question. "Who was she with? I mean, where's her date?

"I don't know," I told him. "I haven't seen him."

"Well, we'd like to talk to him."

"Okay, let me get the membership file."

"I'll get it, Tom," Sherri offered.

She returned a few minutes later with the manila folder that had his name written on top of it. The police took the folder and started reading. "Is this stuff accurate?"

"It should be."

"You mean it better be."

One of the uniformed officers came down from the living room. "He isn't up there."

The detective who had questioned me before started again. "Is it normal for a guy to go off and leave his date here?"

"No, it isn't."

"Okay, let's see if we can find this guy. Try this phone number first, and if that doesn't work, send a car over to this address. Why don't we all go upstairs. I can question the other people while we're waiting."

91

There was very little activity upstairs. Everyone was just sitting around the living room, not even talking. One by one, the detective took the members in the dining room and questioned them. As soon as he was finished with each couple, the two would finish gathering up their belongings and leave. Finally, there was no one left but family.

The police finished the check of all the information in the membership file, and found that the phone was disconnected, a little old lady lived at the address, and instead of having a driver's license number, we had two car licenses. These were checked with Sacramento and found to belong to cars registered in Santa Rosa and Bakersfield.

When the police were getting ready to leave, one of them came over to me. "All I've got to say is that if we ever have to come back here for anything and you don't have accurate records, you're closed, man. That's it, it'll be all over!"

Michael and Janice did a very beautiful thing that afternoon; they made love in the Ballroom. They hoped to revive some of the good vibes the room had before.

The police called later to inform me that the girl died of natural causes; an aneurysm in the head.

Anyone who was not a member of the Retreat had to fill out a guest card that required name, address, phone number, and a driver's license number. All but the license could be phony, but when we started checking licenses, it had to be accurate. Some of the ploys used to try and circumvent the rules were amazing. Everything from guilt trips about our "previous friendship" to outright bribes. I guess one reason I worked the door is because I became very conscientious about the rules after that woman's death.

One Saturday night two nice-looking couples came in the door.

"Good evening. Welcome to Sandstone." I didn't recognize any of them, so I assumed they were guests of another member. Then one of the men informed me he was a member, but hadn't been up for a while. I checked his name in the register, and found that he really was a fully paid-up member.

"Okay, could I have your guests fill out these cards for me, please?" I handed each of them a guest card, noting that both women seemed upset. His date filled out her card after asking him if it was really necessary. The other male filled out his card rapidly, misspelling his street, which showed his nervousness. The last young woman just held hers in her hand. She looked around the room at the forty or so people, then turned to me.

"What kind of place is this, anyway?"

"Didn't he tell you?" I indicated the member.

"No. He just said we were going to a party in a real nice house up in the hills."

I smiled, "Well, that part is obviously true." Then I tuned to the member. "So you didn't tell them?"

"Well, uh…" His face was getting redder by the minute.

"I'll need ten dollars from each guest – if you plan on staying." Sometimes that would give people a convenient excuse to change their mind.

"Oh, I didn't know there would be a charge. Could we talk it over for a minute?"

"Sure, take your time." I knew they wouldn't stay.

"Okay, we'll just go out on the porch." They edged back out the door to let others come in. If it was up to the one girl, they might as well head for the car.

Sure enough, in a few minutes the member came back in – alone. "I don't think we'll be staying. Sorry."

"So am I. It might have helped if you'd been up front about it."

"Yeah, well," he smiled sheepishly, "I'll try that next time." I was sorry they left; two good-looking couples who might have enjoyed themselves if they'd given themselves a chance. I know I would have enjoyed getting to know the one lady.

One thing working the door did was improve my memory of names. It made a nice impression on the members if I called them by name when they arrived – especially the single male members when they brought a date. It was basically the same as walking into a good restaurant and having the maitre d' use your name. It also made the members feel more secure, knowing they weren't just another couple. It wasn't easy because we had over 200 members, but I finally got most of them down. It almost became a game between me and the members; if I didn't greet them by name when they arrived, they'd smile and wait a minute to see if I'd remember. If I didn't, I told them they'd just have to come up more often to I could practice.

Sandstone Retreat had two basic types of membership; one-year for $240.00 or $125.00 initiation fee and $15.00 a month dues. The dues paying members were a problem. Fifteen bucks a month is pocket money for the type of people who belonged to the Retreat, and the great majority kept their dues paid up. But there was that small minority who wanted to see how far they could push us

93

before we demanded payment. We decided they played that game because they lived in a rip-off society and that was standard behavior – how much can I get away with?

Then there was the unpleasant task of cancelling a membership. This was usually done after a group discussion at a Monday night meeting, occasionally it had to be done on the spot. Any family member had permission to do it, but Marty or I usually handled it.

The majority of cancellations were due to the violation of the rule forbidding obnoxious or forceful behavior, and the usual trigger of that behavior was alcohol.

We continually warned people about drinking at the club, but some of them refused to understand. The environment could be extremely volatile on at a Saturday night party, and alcohol had a much faster and stronger effect on some people than they were used to. It was ironic that some people thought they had to drink to give themselves permission, but once they'd drank enough found themselves incapable of doing what they'd drank the booze for. It was a self-defeating process.

There were few cases of physical violence at the Retreat. I think people just felt too vulnerable without their clothes. There were a few times when it looked like a fight might develop, but it took very little persuasion on our part to avert it. The possibility of losing their membership was probably a factor.

There was also the problem of people trying to get a "free ride." We allowed prospective members one free visit before they joined, usually a Wednesday night pot-luck. We tried giving them three visits, but found that it didn't matter – if someone was going to join, they'd do it after one visit. Some people took advantage of the one visit, and decided they'd experienced Sandstone and didn't have to join. We tried to impress upon them that basing their decision on simply attending one party wasn't fair to them, or us, because no two parties were the same. The number of people always changed, the mood that night, they were always different. We didn't want the prospect to make a value judgment based on just that one visit.

One of our beautiful couples, Joe and Melody, walked in the door one night with a guest couple. I knew that the guest couple had been up once before together, and the man had been up once alone. I had to tell Joe and Melody that their guests couldn't stay. The decision wasn't a cheerful one for any of us, especially Melody. But I knew the guest couple had no intention of joining the

Retreat, so I had to deny them entry to a party. Joe and Melody even went to Marty and asked him to override my decision, but it didn't work. The family had an agreement that all of us would support the individual making such a decision, regardless whether we agreed with it or not. There was no way we could be aware of all the circumstances involved in the person's decision, but it would probably be brought up at the next Monday night meeting. Marty did come to me and asked that I reconsider, but I refused. It was quite a scene at the front door, but I felt completely justified in my decision and still do. Joe and Melody found out later that the couple were only interested in talking about alternative lifestyles. They stopped seeing them, but they wrote a letter to John Williamson expressing their displeasure about the way I was running the club. That really hurt. I felt I was doing the right thing. All John said was, "Well, somebody has to do it."

Honor Thy Author

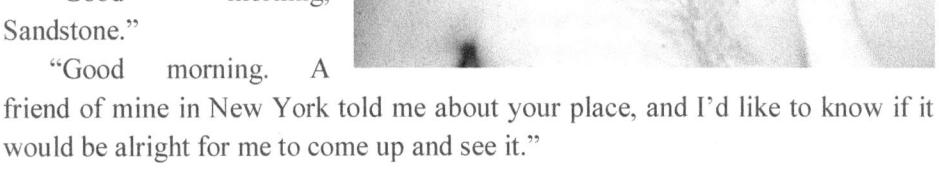

It was exactly one day before I met Nanci that we were first visited by Gay Talese. It was a Saturday morning and I was sitting in the living room on phone duty. It hadn't rung for a while, which was unusual for a Saturday. So when it did, I grabbed it faster than usual.

"Good morning, Sandstone."

"Good morning. A friend of mine in New York told me about your place, and I'd like to know if it would be alright for me to come up and see it."

"Well, first of all, who is your friend and who are you?" It was unusual for someone to call like that and try to wrangle their way to a free party, so we usually checked it out carefully.

95

He told me who his friend was, I knew the name, and that he was Gay Talese. "I'm the author of *Honor Thy Father* and *The Power and the Glory.*"

"Yes, I'm aware of what you've written, Mr. Talese." This wasn't some lightweight hack looking for a sexploitation story. In fact, I didn't know if he was looking for a story at all. "Actually, Mr. Talese..."

"Call me Gay."

"Actually, Gay, we don't usually allow single people at the Retreat on weekends."

"Well, I don't plan on being in town too long. I'm supposed to leave tomorrow night. I just want to come up for a couple of hours this afternoon and see what the place looks like."

"If that's all you're interested in, why don't you come on up?" I gave him directions and hung up.

His afternoon visit lasted ten days. It was interrupted only by an appearance on the *Johnny Carson Show* where Johnny made the mistake of asking, "Well, what's new, Gay?"

He probably expected to hear about Gay's new book, but instead he heard about this beautiful place where Gay had been staying called Sandstone, and about how fantastic it was to walk around nude and not be afraid to touch other people, even be affectionate if they didn't mind.

Johnny took the whole thing pretty well.

Before Gay left, he indicated that this place was so unique, and the eleven of us living there so different, that he just might be interested in writing about us. We thought that was too good to be true, because a number of writers had come to Sandstone to write about us and failed miserably. But here was the country's best and most famous non-fiction writer (by his own admission) telling us he might write about us. Maybe, just maybe, we could finally get an accurate picture out to the world of what we were really trying to do here. We were all excited about the prospect. And the just-filmed movie was also going to be great publicity for Sandstone.

It was toward the end of Gay's first visit that Esquire Magazine wanted to do a story on us. They sent out one of their senior editors, and one of the best photographers in the country, Bert Glenn, who took some fantastic pictures of the interior of the house with people sitting around – one of which appeared in the Magazine. It was one of the best and most representative pictures ever taken at Sandstone.

96

We got a signed contract from the Magazine stating that the story would be written by Gay Talese. Unfortunately, we didn't get Gay's signature on the contract. As it turned out, Gay decided he wasn't ready to write anything about us yet, not even the piddling five-hundred words they wanted to go with the photo. The article did finally appear, but with no by-line. I don't know who actually wrote the article. I do know we were on the verge of telling them to forget the whole thing after all the transcontinental phone calls between Esquire, Gay and Sandstone.

Gay returned to Sandstone in the early Fall, and walked into an entirely different environment from the one he'd left. For one thing, John and Barbara had put the Ranch up for sale – again, and it looked like they had a buyer this time. There had been talk of this among the family members, and a few club members, but it looked serious this time. All of us were pretty shaken. Where would we go? What would we do? None of us looked forward to going back into a society we'd forsaken, and back to a regular job.

The Magazine John had talked about, *Joy*, had faded long ago, but I was trying to rejuvenate it again under the title *Nexus*. We'd received some good material from some of our friends, and I'd done some graphic treatments that we were all happy with. We were even talking to a few people about investing money in the project, and that looked promising.

The plan was that Gay would move in with us, become part of the family, and start doing research on all of us with the "possibility" of a book in mind. He told us it was too early to tell if there really was a book; that would depend on what his research uncovered.

The family was in a quandary. Could Gay write this book? Did he really understand what we were trying to do (there were a few of us who still didn't understand what we were trying to do after living at the Ranch)? It was the topic of more than one Monday night meeting and many private conversations. In the beginning, I believe it was Marty who agreed to cooperate with Gay. The rest of us had doubts about it, especially John and Barbara and myself because of his lack of understanding of the basic philosophy, which became evident one Monday night when we spent hours trying to explain it to him. Unfortunately, it's difficult to make someone understand something that has to be felt. It can't be explained in words, but a person's actions show whether they understand or not.

One thing that bothered us was Gay's attitude toward being part of the family. One Monday night shortly after his return, Sue had made some pretty good cookies (she'd graduated from popcorn), and Gay made us fully aware that he didn't plan on doing any of the work around the place.

"I'm not going to do dishes, or vacuum the carpets, or sweep the driveways, but I am going to pay my way." He explained that he would help buy the groceries, and even pay rent on the room he was sleeping in. As he was talking, he reached out and took two cookies.

I quipped, "Janice, he took two cookies. Put that on his bill." We all laughed, except Gay, but it was an example of his refusal to participate in the lifestyle. Most of his days were spent down the hill playing tennis, because from his viewpoint, there wasn't much happening at the Ranch. He was only interested in interviewing the Williamsons, and the Saturday night parties. But those days were very important to the rest of us.

It turned out that my "two cookies" remark was only the first in a series of personality clashes Gay and I were to have. The fact that Gay Talese was now living at Sandstone caused a lot of interest within the club. Many members had heard of him, and were curious as to why he was here. As manager of the club, so was I. As far as I was concerned, Gay was just another single male at most of the parties he attended, and I wanted to make sure none of the other men felt threatened by him. That was how I noticed he took women into his own bedroom on party nights, leaving their partners to wonder where they were, what they were doing and with whom. That's the breeding ground for fantasies and resentments.

Gay says in his book, "As Sandstone became more prosperous and relaxed about its club operation, a number of preferred people were even admitted as singles, and even given honorary memberships, because their presence suggested an intellectual interest in, if not an endorsement of, the Williamsons' research methods and goals." This may seem to legitimize Gay's attendance at the parties as a single male, but there were never "honorary memberships" granted. He and others, like Alex Comfort, were allowed entry as singles simply because Barbara felt they could benefit Sandstone with publicity. Granted, they both did, but by the time that publicity was out there, the Ranch had been sold. In the meantime, the rest of us had to put up with complaints from club members, and other single males who were turned away, regarding their attendance at parties.

It was standard policy that the family would refrain from taking someone out of the party environment – the main house and the swimming pool – without his or her mate. There was certainly nothing wrong with family members interacting

98

with club members, we encouraged it, but it had to be done within the club environment. If we wanted to take a couple to our private quarters, that was fine, but to take a single out of the environment, meant that their partner was now a single person, and usually a worried one.

When I confronted Gay on his behavior, he became very angry, and accused me of "power tripping" among other things. I was sorry he took it that way, because it reinforced my belief that he did not understand the basics of our philosophy. The whole idea of having intimate relations within the party atmosphere was to destroy the myth that it was something that could only be done in the bedroom with the doors closed and the lights out. Gay was violating that principle. If he brought his own date to the Retreat, he was free to take her any place he wanted, including his bedroom – but not the members.

I walked by his door a few days later and Bunny was nailing a bright silver star on his door, and told me, "That's so all the star fuckers will know where to find him." I asked Bunny how she felt about Gay, and she told me, "He treats women like paper towels; tear one off, use it, and throw it away."

Gay wrote, "A *Goodbar* scene was impossible at Sandstone, where women were protected by those around them from being victims of one man's hostility."

I was sitting upstairs one Saturday night very late, when one of our most beautiful female members sat down beside me. I looked at her and could tell that she was troubled about something. When I asked her about it, she was reluctant to discuss it, but she eventually admitted that she'd been raped downstairs. I immediately wanted to know who it was. She refused to tell me, preferring to not make a scene, but she did say that he was one of Barbara's "honorary" members attending the party as a single male. I quickly ran down the list of single men at the party in my mind, and it was a very short list – there was only one. That was the last party she and her husband attended.

John and Barbara finally agreed to cooperate with Gay on a limited basis, after he told them he could always do the basic research without their help. As far as I know, Barbara Williamson was the only resident female who had sex with Gay, and according to what I read, it was definitely hot sex.

Gay's book was finally published in 1981.

Talese also said, "...it was not until 1974 that a marriage counselor...had acquired enough capital and bank loans to buy Sandstone...that in the interim months had been inactive."

When You're Lonely Enough

It was Monday morning and Barbara and I were in the living room working. "What was wrong with you last night, Tom?" she asked offhandedly.

"What do you mean?"

"I don't know, you just seemed to be on some kind of bad trip."

"Oh. Well, I started feeling lonely yesterday after everyone left, so I decided to take John's advice and explore my feelings. I was lonely, that's all.

Barbara smiled and told me, "Well, I guess when you're lonely enough, you'll do something about it."

At the time, I felt she'd given me a very simplistic answer to a very difficult problem. I've discovered since then that it was one of the most important statements I'd heard in my four years at Sandstone, and that paraphrased, it could apply to a wide range of human problems.

A friend told me once that she was having trouble achieving orgasms, and asked if Sandstone could help. I remembered Barbara's advice to me. "Well, when you want to have an orgasm bad enough, you will." Naturally, she couldn't accept that answer, just as I couldn't accept it when Barbara gave it to me,  but it was the most honest answer I could give her. In other words, take responsibility for your own orgasms.

Shortly after that exchange, I met Nanci, and I thought my loneliness problem was solved for good. She lived with me at Sandstone for all of two months, but they were probably the most memorable two months in all the time I lived there, both from a personal standpoint and also from the community standpoint.

During the first seven weeks of that period, we filmed the Sandstone movie. We also had a special weekend event called "The Emotional Renaissance Faire" with Robert Rimmer (see his Introduction to this book) and the "Nine Day Growth Experience" led by Ralph Yaney and Lucy Claggett.

I first met Nanci on a Sunday afternoon in late May. Her father, Dale, was a member, and brought her up to see the place. I'd gone downstairs to see if anyone left wanted to shoot some pool, and she was leaning against the table. Just as I smiled and said hello, Dale came over and formally introduced us.

She was a very beautiful girl with a near-perfect body enhanced by her erect posture. Dale assured me she was eighteen. I racked the balls on the pool table, and took a few shots. I asked her, "Would you like to play?"

"Oh, I'm not very good. Thanks anyway." She didn't seem interested in shooting pool or anything else. I couldn't tell whether she was frightened by the environment or just bored. I took a few more shots, and kept an eye on her while I moved around the table – which was easy, she was a visual treat. She seemed a little nervous. She kept glancing over at the bar where her father was talking to a few other people, but she made no move to join him.

"My father said you run this place. Is that true?"

"Well, it's partly true. Actually, I'm only one of ten people who operate the Retreat."

"I don't understand."

I put my cue stick back in the rack and turned my attention to her. "Would you like to talk about it? I'd like to get your opinion on a couple of things."

"Like what?" she asked, slightly nervous but curious.

"I'm interested in finding out what young people think of this type of place and the activity that goes on here."

"Well…okay. What do you want to know?" She was still keeping an eye on her dad.

"Maybe it would be better if we went someplace else to talk. How about coming up to my office? It's much quieter there."

"Yeah, that sounds like a good idea. It's kind of difficult to concentrate in here." She immediately started for the side door walking right past her father and his friends without saying a word.

We walked up the driveway to the office, and I took the opportunity to enjoy the lovely day and the lovely young woman walking beside me. She seemed to be someplace else entirely. She didn't turn her head as we passed the swimming pool, just kept looking straight ahead or down at the ground.

When we got to the office, she sat in a chair and I took the desk chair. When I looked at her, I had the flash of a student sitting in the principal's office.

"What did you want to talk about?" Her tone was a little defensive, and she sat with her legs crossed, standard female pose, with a look of aloofness that was betrayed by other signs of nervousness.

"As I said before, I'm interested in finding out how young people feel about Sandstone, Nanci. Maybe you have some thoughts about it. I have a theory that young people have more trouble handling this experience than people over thirty. What do you think?"

"About what?"

"About what I just said."

"Um, I don't know. Seems like a nice place. Kind of hard to tell in a short visit." Her eyes kept wandering around the room, not staying on one thing long enough to really see it.

I kept trying to get her to open up without success until I asked, "How do you feel about your father coming here?"

"I don't have anything to do with that. He does what he wants, and I do what I want."

"Why did he bring you here?"

At that she almost laughed out loud. "I think he wants me to be a Swinger – like him."

"How do you feel about that?"

She took a long drag on her cigarette before answering. "I don't mind if he wants to do it, but it's not for me."

"You don't like Swinging?"

"Not much."

We talked some more, and she opened up a little bit about her life and her friends and what their social life was like.

"Do you and your friends ever use drugs?"

"Oh, no! I'd never get into that kind of crowd." Too quick an answer.

"Hey, listen, since your dad's a member here, I want you to know that you're free to come up anytime you feel like it. The membership is kind of a family thing. So if you feel like coming up and going for a swim some afternoon, just come on up. Okay?"

"Really? Yeah, that's not a bad idea. There's not much to do where I am now."

"Good. I've got some work to finish, but I want to thank you for spending time with me. Maybe I'll see you later." With that, I got up and escorted her to the door, then we returned to the house.

The following Friday morning I saw her again. I was in the office working on a hand-lettered menu for the upcoming Rimmer weekend. We planned to initiate our new kitchen John had built with the help of some of the family. We planned on serving a variety of sandwiches and soft drinks. Doug was busy down the hill buying food for the crowd we expected to visit. It was a busy time for all of us.

This weekend was also the start of filming of the Sandstone movie to be produced and directed by Jonathan and Bunny Dana. They first came to Sandstone in 1971. A friend of theirs, Ron, had heard about the Retreat while on a business trip in New York. They'd just finished making a movie called, Darkness, Darkness, and he was discussing distribution with a company. The man told him they might check out this place in Los Angeles.

They had written Sandstone asking for literature, and after reading it, thought it might be a good idea to visit in person. The three of them came up that warm weekend to find out what the place was all about. At the time, Bunny was very much in love with both Ron and Jonathan, and they had a nice life up in Palo Alto. Sandstone changed all that.

Ron met Marty's partner, Mag, and it was instant love. In fact, Mag ended up leaving Sandstone with Ron. Jonathan met a woman named Nancy, and it was almost the same thing. During all of this, Marty was begging Bunny to comfort him. "Me comfort you? Jesus Christ, Marty, you live here! This is the first time I've been here and I'm watching both the men I love drift away. If anybody needs some comforting, I'm first in line!"

That was the beginning of the Sandstone movie. They started working on the arrangements, and Jonathan moved to Sandstone in December of 1971, just a few months after me. Bunny joined him later, after finishing a conference in Washington D.C. on free clinics. They became the last two members of the community to move in, and there was little room for them. They had to crowd in the small bedroom that Albert had used in the main house. It adjoined a bathroom that was open to the members, so their nights, especially Wednesday and Saturday, were constantly interrupted by the flush of the toilet and the running of the shower.

103

Raising money for the movie took longer than planned, and that led to occasional talks of forgetting the whole thing. But in the late Spring of 1972 we watched them interviewing prospective cameramen, soundmen and various other people who were going to be involved in this major undertaking.

The family's excitement about the Rimmer weekend was now doubled by the start of filming taking place at the same time. We were all looking forward to the film, but with some apprehension. They were actually going to produce a full-length documentary movie about us. After a year of raising the money, it was finally going to happen!

Nanci came into the office where I was working on the menu that Friday morning and greeted me with a big smile. She was definitely more relaxed than her first visit, and we talked for about an hour about her and the weekend ahead. She told me she was a nurse in the supply room of a local hospital, and that she wanted to specialize in burn patients. Finally, she got up to leave.

"Make yourself at home, Nanci, you're my guest…for as long as you like."After she left, I went back to work on the menu and other projects I had to finish for Saturday. Every now and then I'd go down to the main house for a cup of coffee, and to discuss something with John or Marty. Each time I sat down in the living room, Nanci would come over and sit very close to me as if she really belonged there. I ventured touching her a couple of times, and instead of moving away, she actually moved in closer. I put my arm around her shoulders. She even brought me a sandwich when I was back in the office, and sat with me while I ate it. There was little doubt in my mind that we enjoyed each other's company.

I lost track of her in the afternoon when I got busy with last-minute details, and I didn't see her until I came down for dinner. She was sitting on one of the couches, so I went over and kissed her on top of her head. She turned around and gave a very warm smile. "Let's eat, okay?" I took her hand and led her into the kitchen to get dinner. We sat close to each other and didn't talk while we ate. After dinner we sat in the living room with some of the other family members and talked about the upcoming invasion for a while. Then I said, "I'm tired. Want to go to the cottage?" Without saying anything, she got up and we left.

We made our way down the path to the cottage and went in. As soon as I got inside, I started undressing. I was very glad to see Nanci doing the same thing. We both jumped on my queen-size waterbed that took up most of the floor space and made love.

It wasn't the greatest sex I've ever had, but it was good. She seemed to like cuddling very close to me almost as much as she appeared to like it when I entered her. Surprise! Someone had been there shortly before me. We talked about it afterwards, and she admitted that it had been Marty. Good old Marty. He found someone to console him. Of course, he always did have a thing for newcomers, especially young ones. Right now I didn't care. Nanci and I were very happy with each other and went to sleep curled in each other's arms.

I awoke Saturday morning to watch Nanci putting on her swimsuit bottom (which became her standard mode of dress). "Good morning, Tom. I'm going for a swim. Want to join me?"

"Sure. Just give me a minute to wake up." Finally, I rolled off the bed, grabbed two towels, gave her one with a kiss, and we walked out the door.

It was a beautiful day! The birds were singing, the sun was bright and warm and I had my arm around a beautiful young woman. What could be better!

As we walked toward the pool, I noticed representatives from The Happy Company, our co-sponsors for the weekend, busy placing brightly colored banners around the main house and in the trees. We waved to each other.

"Wow!" Nanci exclaimed, "This place is really starting to look good."

"Yes, I think it's going to be a fun weekend." Of course, I was thinking of more than just the social event; I had my own fantasy working, and it involved Nanci.

We took a short swim, showered together, then went down to the main house and had a bite to eat while we sat in the living room coordinating the day's activities. I would spend most of the day working at the registration desk up on the entrance road. Nanci offered her services in the kitchen, and Doug readily accepted. I picked up one of the walkie-talkies we were going to use for communication. Nanci kissed me good-bye and it felt like we'd been together for weeks. We were a team and we both knew it.

The crowd started arriving before noon, and I was kept busy signing people in. Since Sandstone is a private club, it's necessary for people attending the "Faire" to fill out a temporary membership application for the Retreat. Most of them did so without questions, but a few who wouldn't sign the form – no good reason, they just refused to sign. Even when I told them they wouldn't be allowed on the premises, they still refused. So I had no choice but to turn them away.

105

Occasionally, Jon and Bunny would bring a cameraman and soundman up to film some of the activity. That had two effects: it made some people even more paranoid or it made the event more interesting to the really curious.

I spent almost all day at the registration desk. Nanci came up to see me a few times, but spent most of the day in the kitchen. Feeding that many people wasn't an easy task. Doug needed all the help he could get. He did all the cooking, but there was a lot of prep and serving.

When I finally closed down registration late in the afternoon and returned to the main house, the first thing I did was check downstairs. I couldn't believe it! There were so many sleeping bags on the floor there was hardly room to walk without stepping on them. Obviously, there were going to be a lot of people spending the night. Since most of them had never attended a Sandstone party, it should be interesting.

Bob Rimmer spoke on the front lawn in the afternoon, in a swimsuit, and promised to continue the rap session downstairs after dinner. I found Nanci in the kitchen and told her we'd work the bar downstairs during the party. There were so many newcomers tonight I thought it might keep the alcohol consumption down if we were behind the bar dispensing it. Actually, it was a good place to observe a party. We had a good view of the whole room, people came to the bar to get drinks and talk, and we could see who was going in the Ballroom – and how long they stayed. It was a voyeur's delight.

The dialogue between Rimmer and the club and guests was great. He learned a few things about himself, and about the Sandstone people, and they found out a lot about a writer of fiction. The main topic of discussion boiled down to recreational sex, and just about everybody had a different viewpoint on it. But I believe the consensus was that they'd like it very much if they could live in a society that allowed people the freedom to act on their feelings as long as they were willing to take the consequences of those acts, and that included sex.

When Bob Rimmer finished his discussion, the party really got started. There was still a lot of conversation, but there was also dancing in the light show, massaging, touching and plenty of sex. Many of these people had never experienced sex in front of a large group of people – or even just one spectator – but the sandstone regulars were quick to introduce them to the experience. Not all of them joined in; I saw more than one person climb into their sleeping bag and pull it up over their head.

Some time after midnight, Nanci and I returned to the cottage. We were both tired, but not too tired to pass up an opportunity for some sex. Once again, it was good but not great. For one thing, she hadn't had an orgasm either time we'd made love. There could be any number of reasons for that, but it did bother me.

Sunday dawned even clearer and warmer than Saturday. We went over to the house and started our second day together. We had arranged for Marty and Sue to relieve me at the registration after a few hours so I could take some photos of the activities. Jon and Bunny and their film crew were also preparing to shoot some more film. It was too nice a day and there were too many beautiful people to pass up an opportunity to take some good photos.

There was a lady in the shallow end of the pool leading a group in an exercise called "Passing the Warm." This involved a group of people getting introduced to touching each other. It ended with them forming two rows and passing a floating person along between them. Some really warm, sensual photos were taken of that excrcise.

There was also a class in sensual massage going on downstairs, similar to the Von Neumann technique, that also offered some good pictures. A couple of group conversations were discussing different aspects of alternative lifestyles. It was exciting to see and hear people discussing these topics.

All in all, Sunday was a busy day. Nanci and I spent some time together, but we were apart also because of the different activities. I do know the two of us went for a swim at some point, and ended up making love in the pool – in front of about thirty surprised people. We were in love and nothing bothered us. We certainly weren't ashamed of it.

Later that night, after everyone had left, the family gathered in the living room to talk about the weekend. Nanci and I knew it was time for her to leave, but we kept putting it off. She had to be at work the next morning, and I would be busy cleaning up the mess left by over two hundred people.

Nanci leaned over and whispered, "Tom, I don't really want to leave."

"Yeah, I know. But I do think it's best."

"I mean I don't want to leave ever."

"Okay, but that's going to require some thinking on both our parts, Nanci. Moving in here is a very big step for someone."

"But that's what I want. Don't you?"

"I…think so. But I want to make sure. Go home and come back up Tuesday after work. We'll talk about it then. You need time down the hill and I need time here."

I kissed her and felt the tears on her cheeks. Why didn't I just tell her to stay? It would have been so easy. But I didn't. She kissed each of the family members good-bye, and I walked her to her car. "I'll see you Tuesday. Right?"

"Okay, Tom, but I'm not going to change my mind." One last kiss, and she drove off.

The following week was especially hectic. Jon and Bunny's film crew invaded the Ranch en masse, commandeered the North House, and proceeded to turn the living room of the main house into a sound stage. There were bright lights everywhere, cables strung out like black spaghetti, sound blankets stapled to the ceiling and godawful orange gels put on all the windows. The crew consisted of two cameramen, a soundman, a production assistant (known as a "Gofer"), an assistant cameraman, and a grip. This gang was augmented by others when the shooting schedule required additional help. There was no doubt about it – we were making a movie!

Nanci did come back up Tuesday after work, and spent the night with me. Neither of us had changed our minds, so it was taken for granted she'd move in. She continued going down the hill every morning to go to work, but she spent every night at the Ranch. It felt good to have someone living with me after I'd been looking so long.

The following Monday night at the first meeting they filmed, we announced that Nanci was part of the family. The news was met with happiness by everyone. Barbara asked her how much longer she planned on working, and Nanci told her, "I gave my two-week notice today." That was fine with us, because we didn't feel it was a good idea to live at the Ranch and work down the hill. It was a serious conflict of value systems.

None of the film crew had been to Sandstone before their initial interview, and had no idea what went on there. It didn't take them long to find out. They tried to maintain their professional air, but it was difficult when they were surrounded by beautiful naked bodies. They were mostly single young men, with the exception of one, and his wife was in San Francisco. She did come down to join him later, but he, like the rest of the crew, was a single male in the candy store.

They planned to shoot everything that happened at the Ranch over the next seven weeks, that they meant everything. So after Nanci's introduction at the Monday night meeting, we returned to the cottage and there was a knock on the door before we even got in bed. "Come in!"

It was Jonathan. "Hi, Tom. Can we come in?" Without waiting for an answer, he and three more people crowded into the small room. One of the guys took the light bulb out of the overhead socket, and replaced it with a much brighter photo flood, while the others were busy setting up camera, microphone and tape recorder. "We'd like to talk to you about tonight. Okay?"

I laughed. "Do we have a choice?" By this time, the camera and tape recorder were both spinning.

Jonathan asked, "Tom, what did you think of the meeting tonight?"

"Well, I wouldn't call it a meeting so much as a nice, friendly get-together. Definitely not the normal Monday night meeting."

"Why do you say that?"

"I think the whole night would have been different without the lights, camera and mikes. It's pretty obvious, to us at least, that the family is a little intimidated by all that stuff."

"How about you?"

"Sure, me too. Not so much the camera, but definitely the tape recorder."

"Do you think we'll be able to film a real Monday night meeting?"

I thought about it a minute, well aware of the tape recorder. "I don't know, Jon. I doubt it. Marty isn't about to loosen up in front of the camera, and I'm not sure John would let him – or me, for that matter."

"How could John stop you?"

"He controls that meeting, Jon. If he doesn't want something discussed, or if he wants the topic changed, it happens. You have to remember that this is John and Barbara's trip and we all are aware of that. They have final say on everything, and that includes whether we stay here, and the Monday night meetings."

"Nanci, how did you feel about the meeting?"

"I was kind of bored. There just wasn't much happening."

"How does it feel to be part of the family?"

She brightened. "I like it. I feel like I've found what I was looking for."

"Okay, we'll let you guys get some sleep. Thanks for the interview, and Nanci, I'd like to say I'm glad you're part of the family." With that, Jon and his crew departed.

We made love after they left, and once again, it was enjoyable, but Nanci didn't have an orgasm. That was beginning to really bother me, and I was beginning to question her feelings about sex. One afternoon later in the week, I found out.

I'd gone down on her, then we had intercourse. After we finished, we lay beside each other on the bed. She said, "Tom, would you do me a favor?"

"Sure, babe, what is it?"

"Well, after you do that, would you mind washing your face?"

I didn't know what to say. No woman had ever made that request, and I'd gone down on quite a few. It caught me completely off guard, so I just let it drop.

During the next few weeks we talked a lot, and had sex two or three times a day, but Nanci still didn't have an orgasm. A couple of times she seemed right on the verge, but never got all the way there. She seemed to enjoy the sex we had, and never complained about her lack of orgasms. She asked me about my past relationships, and I told her briefly about Pamela and a few other women I'd known since moving to Sandstone. I told her that Pamela was on a cross-country trip, and would be back for a while. She'd taken all four children with her, but Brandi left the group in Texas. Pam called me about that time and asked if I was still living alone. When I told her no, she hung up on me.

I also told Nanci about Camille who had first come to Sandstone on a warm summer day with her friend, Corinne, who was interested in having us publish her book of poetry. I met them at the door, and was immediately over-whelmed by the warm, friendly person Corinne introduced me to. Camille gave me an unexpected kiss.

We sat in the living room talking for a while, and when it became evident that Corinne and I would be talking business, Camille asked for directions to the front lawn. I gave them to her, and she gave me another warm smile as she left.

110

Corinne and I continued talking about her book of poetry. At some point, I went into the kitchen for another cup of coffee. On the way back I made a point of walking close to the glass door so I could look out at the lawn. Camille was lying on her back, nude, and from where I was standing, I could see that she had a beautiful slim figure with small breasts and lovely red hair. She was very nice to look at and she was definitely female.

I returned to the couch and chatted a few minutes before suggesting that we take advantage of the beautiful day and join Camille on the lawn. Corinne quickly agreed.

I picked a spot between the two women, but a little closer to Camille. Corinne was sharp enough to see where my interest was, and quietly concentrated on getting some sun while I started talking to her lovely friend with the fantastic body and hair that looked even better with the sun shining through it.

She told me about her husband and three children, I complemented her on maintaining such a lovely figure after birthing three children, and explained a little about Sandstone. All the time I talked, I looked at her, and finally asked if she objected to being touched. She replied that she didn't mind a bit – in fact she enjoyed it. So I reached over and touched her. It didn't take long for us to admit that we were both very turned on.

"Why don't you show me your cottage, Tom?"

I replied, "What's wrong with this beautiful house right behind us? It's much closer."

"I'd really rather go to your cottage."

So I took her to my cottage, and we made love. It was one of the most joyful experiences either of us ever had. When it was finished, we could do nothing but lie close to each other and smile. It was as if we'd both been holding back waiting for this time together. The orgasms we experienced were far more than we'd had before.

After a while, she rolled over and boldly told me, "I give the best head in the world and I want to prove it to you."

I laughed, "You expect me to object?" By the time the last word was out of my mouth, my cock was in hers and she wasn't lying; it was the best I'd ever had. Then she stopped and asked, "Don't you want to come?"

"Very much so!"

111

So she continued. It took a while, but I did finally have an orgasm – not a really big one, but it felt great. When we relaxed again, I told her it was the first orgasm I'd achieved with fellatio in over seven years.

"You're kidding!"

"I wish I was."

"How come?"

"The woman I was living with for the past seven years refused to let me have an orgasm when she gave me head – which wasn't often."

"That female is weird!"

"Probably, but thanks for ending a very long drought."

That was Camille. We saw each other a few more times. I drove down to her home in the Valley and brought her up to the Retreat. On one trip up the winding back road, we were listening to the radio and suddenly a song came on that hit us both so hard I had to pull over and stop just to listen to it – "The First Time Ever I Saw Your Face" by Roberta Flack. She surprised me by sending a beautiful card with a feather and a leaf inside. The words said;

A falling leaf,
A soaring bird,
These things will always
Remind me of you.

It was the most tender expression of feelings that happened during my time at Sandstone.

Unfortunately, our relationship became a serious threat to her husband (he didn't understand the concept of Satellite Relationships), so we decided to back off. We loved each other, but there were others to be considered, specifically, the three children.

Nanci seemed truly interested when I told her about Camille and the others (I didn't list *all* of them), and responded by telling me about her past. She told me about her alcoholic mother who kept a couple of pill bottles handy, and had died in a fire she started by falling asleep with a lit cigarette in her hand (Flashback; "I want to specialize in burn patients"). She'd been raped at some early age, and there had been a year-long marriage to a Hispanic named Joe her step-mother hated, and insisted Nanci's dad kick her out of the house if she didn't stop seeing the guy, so she married him. She was obviously under-age at the time, so did her dad approve the marriage? I never found out.

She also told me about her brother, and how she was always jealous of him because her dad spent more time with him and showed him more affection. All in all, her history was pretty sordid and unhappy. This surprised me, because so much of what she told me contradicted things she revealed when we first met – like finding out she was no stranger to drugs.

During the filming of the movie, Jonathan interviewed Nanci and her father. "Dale, how do you feel about your daughter living here at Sandstone?"

"I think it's fantastic!" he replied. "Of course, I don't think of her as my daughter exactly – more like a beautiful, young female."

"Nanci, was he a good father?"

"No."

The first four weeks of our relationship were beautiful. We spent a lot of time together, but we didn't shirk our responsibilities at the Ranch. The movie was being filmed, and we never knew when or where the camera and microphone might show up.

Then one Sunday evening, Nanci had her first orgasm, and it was a real body-wrenching, tear-jerking orgasm. I'd been going down on her and felt her get right to the edge, but not go all the way. So I began changing things; I'd go down on her for a few minutes, then when she started reacting, I'd switch to intercourse. When she started responding to that, I'd switch back to cunnilingus. I did this three or four times before she finally lost control and had the orgasm.

"Wow!" she exclaimed. "I guess that was an orgasm."

"Yeah...I think that's what it was." We both seemed very happy and tired after that, and went to sleep pretty early.

Two nights later, we tried again, but she wouldn't let go. She cried and screamed, "Help me!", but there was nothing I could do. She simply wouldn't have another orgasm. That was the last time we had sex.

The turn-off was slow but sure. She started her period two days later, and she'd always been reluctant to have sex during her period. I didn't notice anything until a week later when she just didn't get turned on. My advances would be gently repulsed, and she spent more time away from me. Most of the time was spent at the North House where she'd lie out on the patio to get some sun and talk to the film crew.

I tried to talk about it, but she refused to admit there was a problem. All she'd say was that maybe she was just going through a phase, that it had happened before, and not to worry. She'd get turned back on again. But she didn't. The final straw was when I found out she'd had sex with one of the film crew, and I confronted her about it.

"You're jealous!"

"No, Nanci, I'm not jealous. I've looked at it from all sides and if anything, I'm envious. I'm not upset about what you did with Kit, any more than I was upset when you had sex with Marty. What I'm upset about is what you're *not* having sex with me. If our relationship was as strong as it was two weeks ago, it wouldn't make any difference. Except I might wonder why you're having sex with a guy who is simply using you."

"No, he's not, Tom! I thought that was what this place was all about – having the freedom to do what you want to do."

"That's true, Nanci. But another aspect of that freedom is being ready to accept the consequences. And that's what you're doing now."

"What?"

"You're finding out what the consequences are."

"Well…let me think about it. I'm confused." She adopted a hurt-little-girl expression I hadn't seen before.

There was some resentment expressed within the family about all the time she was spending away from the main house, and neglecting to help out, but there was nothing I could do about that. If they had a problem with her, they should bring it up at the next Monday night meeting. I wasn't going to try and explain why she preferred the company of the film crew instead of the family, but she did. Sue went up to get her once in a while, but I refused. At that point in our relationship, it would appear as if I was checking up on her.

Her behavior only got worse. She stayed away from me and slept with Kit. She went down the hill with him to shows and didn't get back until three in the morning. I put up with it for a few days, but I finally had to do something about it. When she walked in the cottage about two in the morning, I brought the subject up again. "Nanci, what do you expect from me?"

"Nothing," she mumbled, lying in bed with her back to me.

"That's not true, babe."

"Yes, it is, Tom. I don't expect anything from you. Just leave me alone." She was obviously irritated.

114

"Nanci, let me tell you what your expectations are. You expect to live at Sandstone in this cottage, be supported by the community, and do exactly what you want without taking me or the community into consideration. You expect me to let you continue living here as my partner, without doing any work on our relationship. Those are your expectations, and I, and the family, can't accept them."

Without turning around, she just said, "So?"

"So I think it's time for you to decide what you're going to do, because I can't continue this way. Either we're going to have a primary relationship, or we'll have to make other arrangements."

"You mean like me moving out of the cottage?" She finally sounded serious.

"That's one option, thought I'm not sure John or the rest of the family would buy that. You moved in here as my partner with the intention of building a relationship, not as a single individual moving into a community that's supposed to provide an environment where couples can work together to make their relationships better."

At that, she turned over and looked at me. "Look, I'm just having a little trouble right now. I'll be okay, just wait until they finish shooting the movie and things get back to normal. It'll be okay."

"Nanci, this is normal. It doesn't matter whether they're shooting a movie or anything else. Whatever is happening here is normal." When she heard that, she rolled back over and appeared to go to sleep.

About three hours later I was still trying to sleep. I just couldn't turn my head off. There had to be some way to get through to her, because I still loved her and didn't want to break up. I was laying on my side thinking about it when she moved and our fingers touched. That was all it took to get me turned on. I very slowly started moving my fingers on hers, and she responded by moving her hand closer so that I could touch her whole hand. Then our toes touched, and I moved my foot until our legs were touching from the knees down. By now, I had an enormous erection and began moving the rest of my body closer. She responded by turning enough that I was touching her breast, and most of her body was touching mine. She was moving her torso in a very turned-on manner. God, what torture! Finally, after minutes of this intimate touching and reading all her signs, I put my hand on her pubic area. She responded by lifting her buttocks off the bed in eager anticipation. But when I put my arm around her waist and started pulling her to me, she gave a very grouchy moan and pulled away. She turned back over and moved out of reach. There was no way I could put up with this!

A few days later I talked to Nanci again. I told her about the other night, and all she said was that she was asleep and didn't remember anything about it. I told her I believed her, but it didn't change anything. It was still an impossible situation that had to change. I couldn't do my work properly, and she wasn't doing much work at all, preferring to spend her time at the North House with the film crew. Neither of us was donating much time or effort to the community. I told her it was time to bring it in front of the family, and ask for help in resolving the situation.

"You mean next Monday night?"

"No, I can't wait that long. We have the right to call a special meeting if we feel it's critical, and I feel this really is."

"Okay, I'll do anything that will help." Obviously that wasn't exactly true. We talked about the meeting and what might happen for the rest of the day. I tried to explain how the process worked, and that it was the only method I knew of to resolve the situation.

"When are you going to do it, Tom?"

"I don't see any reason to wait, so I'll do it in the morning." We were lying in bed, it was after midnight, and we'd been talking about the meeting for hours. I warned her that the family would probably have some critical things to say to both of us.

"Like what"

"Well, I handled things wrong in the last few weeks and I know it."

"What kind of things?"

"Like trying to put you on a dependency trip, Nanci. You're a pretty independent person, and I tried to make you dependent on me so you'd want to stay with me. It didn't work, but I never should have tried in the first place."

The next morning Nanci and I got up about eight o'clock and walked to the main house. Nobody else was up yet, so I told Nanci to wait in the living room while I rounded them up. First, I went to Jon and Bunny's door. Jon answered it.

"I'm calling a special meeting this morning. Can you and Bunny come to the living room?"

"Can we film it?"

I thought about that for a minute, the influence it would have. "I'll leave that up to you." Then I went to the other houses and woke up the rest of the family.

116

After finishing that, I returned to the living room and waited for everyone to get there.

Jon and Bunny had brought a cameraman and a soundman, but neither of them were doing anything. There seemed to be a wait-and-see attitude.

All of a sudden, John and Barbara got up and walked out of the house. I didn't know where they were

"What are we waiting for, Tom?" Marty asked.

"John and Barbara."

"Where'd they go?"

"I don't know. I'll see if I can find them." I left the house and saw Barbara standing outside the swimming pool, so I headed there. I wasn't aware of the film crew following me. As I approached, John came out of the pool building.

I asked, "Hey, what's happening?"

"You've got a circus rigged down there, Tom, and we don't want any part of it."

"What? John, all I'm doing is asking you and the rest of the family for some help. Nanci and I can't resolve it ourselves, so we agreed to bring it up in front of the whole community."

"I don't see that, Tom. I see you asking us to condemn Nanci, to act as your judge, for the purpose of forcing Nanci to have a relationship with you, and I refuse to be put in that position." Actually, that isn't what we had planned at all. Nanci and I had talked about it, and come to the conclusion that she was going to have to find someplace else at the Ranch to live, or she'd have to leave. We'd reached the point of "irreconcilable differences." The meeting was to determine if there was anyplace else she could live at the Ranch. This whole confrontation was being filmed, and did end up in the movie. Jonathan dropped the ball by not following up on our feelings about it.

I was dumbfounded. I didn't know what to do. I felt cheated by John and Barbara, because I was trying to work within their philosophy, and they weren't letting me. I resented the fact that they didn't understand that Nanci and I had talked it over, and agreed on this course of action. I felt they really underestimated me. I stood for a minute, trying to think of what to do next. Finally, I just said, "Well, John, I guess somebody is always trying to lay a trip on somebody else." I returned to the house without explaining who I thought was laying a trip on whom.

I walked in and told Nanci to join me outside.

117

Marty asked, "What's happening, Tom?"

"There's not going to be a meeting, Marty." I turned to the rest of the family. "I apologize for waking all of you up."

"Why not?" Marty insisted.

"John and Barbara refuse to attend." I just wanted to get the hell out of the house.

"Well, let's have the meeting anyway," Marty said. "We don't need them."

"Yes, we do, Marty." Nanci and I left the house and walked down to the front lawn.

"What now, Tom?"

"Well, I guess it's up to us – which is where it's always been. We just have to work it out between us."

Things didn't change the rest of that week. John talked to Nanci a couple of times, and asked her why she never took off the swimsuit bottom.

"Because I've got pimples on my butt, and it's embarrassing."

"Bullshit. You know as well as I do that exposure to the sun and air would be one of the best things for that. I think you can't take them off because you hate your vagina."

"What?"

"You heard me."

"Well, I don't agree with you."

"Okay, then, take them off." They were sitting beside each other on a couch, and Nanci lifted up enough to pull the swimsuit bottoms down.

"Okay, so now what?"

"Nothing," John replied. "Let's see if you keep them off."

Other than that small clothing change, her behavior was the same until Saturday. I was sitting in the cottage doing some text editing, and Nanci had gone over to the main house. I heard John and Barbara's car drive away, but took little notice of it because they often went up to the motor home during the day for a nap.

About an hour later, I finished the editing job and walked over to the house for another cup of coffee. When I got there, I looked around for Nanci, but she wasn't there. I even checked downstairs. When I asked Sue if she'd seen her, she told me Nanci had been talking to John earlier, but she didn't know where she was now.

The only thing I could think was that maybe she went up the hill with John and Barbara to talk to her like they said they would. John had said that what she needed most was to masturbate to orgasm, and have a warm, loving relationship with another female. Maybe they were working on that.

I got my coffee and headed back toward the cottage. As I passed the swimming pool, I saw Nanci. She was coming from the North House and Kit wasn't too far behind her. She took the upper path down to the cottage, and he came toward the pool. I ignored him and walked over to the cottage. She was coming out of the bathroom just as I entered.

"You're not trying very hard, Nanci."

She didn't say anything, just turned to leave, heading for the main house. I sat for a minute, trying to calm down, but I couldn't. If only she'd been up the hill with...

I went over to the house and found her in the kitchen. "Nanci, we've got to talk dammit!"

She stopped. "Alright, Tom," she said resignedly.

"I'm going back over to the cottage. Please come over when you finish here."

"Okay."

I got another cup of coffee and returned to the cottage. I waited over a half-hour, but she didn't show. Where the hell was she? Back up at the North House? My head was spinning. Finally, I couldn't stand it any longer, and returned to the main house. I found her out on the terrace with Sue and somebody I didn't recognize.

Forgetting the possibility that the other person might be a prospective member, I said, "Look, little girl, I'm through playing games! Either get your ass over to the cottage or decide where you're going to be sleeping tonight!" I left without waiting for an answer.

It was a long time before she finally came through the door, and when I saw her, I could tell she was on the verge of hysterics. She'd been crying. "Okay, Tom, you win. We'll do it your way. I'm moving out of the cottage."

"What?" What do you mean? That's not my way. I want you to stay and work on our relationship."

"The hell you do. Besides, it's already been decided. John told me to move in with Janice for a while."

I was dumbfounded – again. What the hell was going on? And why couldn't John have told me?

119

So Nanci moved out of the cottage, but not out of Sandstone.

Separation

After Nanci moved out of the cottage, things started happening almost faster than I could keep track of them.

John and Barbara and I were sitting in the living room one evening talking about Nanci, and they asked me what I thought would be the best approach. I told them any effort to help her on my part was futile because she refused to believe anything I told her. So if anyone was going to help her, it would have to be the Williamsons or the rest of the community. They asked me where she was, and I told them she was downstairs listening to music. They suggested I get her and we could talk.

I went downstairs and found her lying on a mattress near the stereo. When I told her John and Barbara wanted to talk to her, the reaction was irritation, like she resented being interrupted just to listen to more bullshit, but she came back upstairs with me.

She sat down next to John and Barbara. John asked her if she'd thought about the situation.

"Well, I have, but I can't decide what to do," she told him.

"Nanci, it would help if you could answer these two questions: why can't you have a relationship with Tom? Why do you want to have sex without having orgasms?"

She thought for a minute. "I just can't answer those questions." Then she made the mistake of adding, "As a matter of fact, I was thinking of going back to school, and that would mean leaving here."

That's all it took. Barbara immediately told her, "Start packing. You can leave tomorrow."

"Now wait a minute," I said, "I've got something to say about this. Look, Nanci has moved out of the cottage, so let's see how this arrangement works for a little while. Nanci, I'm not telling you to move back in the cottage as long as we can at least be friends; as long as the relationship isn't destructive to the rest of the community. Let's see if we can work it through. Think about it," I told her, "You're 18-years old, and you have a chance to make a quantum leap in personal

120

growth. If you stick it out and work on this, you can be in a place most people never get to, and the few that do are already in their forties. You've told me you're strong, so let's see if you really are."

That encounter happened about a week before John and Barbara and Marty and Sue climbed into the motor home and headed north for a vacation. They said they'd be gone about two or three weeks. Jon and Bunny had finished their shooting schedule, and also decided to take a short vacation before starting the editing process. That left me, Nanci, Doug and Janice to run the place.

I had expressed some concerns about this a few days before they left, and he said, "Tom, if I didn't have complete confidence in your ability to handle this thing, we wouldn't be going."

That made me feel a little better, but I was still worried. They left on a Wednesday evening, and the following Friday Dr. Yaney's group-living experience was to start. At the time, I didn't expect that to be much of a hassle, but it was one more thing I had to consider. It was bound to require some time and energy from the four of us, and I could only hope we would have a little extra to give.

Things started off badly, and got considerably worse by the weekend. Nanci practically refused to talk to me, and I couldn't get through to Janice. She and Doug were still trying to "distance" from each other, and the 9-day group thing proved to be more complicated than we had originally planned. By Saturday, even the members started noticing the extremely bad vibes in the house and a few of them talked to me about it. My head was so overloaded with input by then that I wasn't too nice telling them we had some problems we were working on. I kept hoping and praying John would call so I could ask his advice, but by Sunday, it was evident he wasn't going to. This was our trip, and we were the ones who would have to get it straightened out. I decided it was time to sit down and take a long look at the whole mess.

The situation among the four of us was, to my knowledge, unique in the history of Sandstone. It was the first time both members of a broken pair bond had continued living in the environment. Before, one or both members had moved out. Now, we had four individuals instead of two pair bonds. The situation was made worse by the mutual animosity all four of us were exhibiting. I wanted Nanci to either respect her original commitment or move out. I could see no way I could co-exist with her at Sandstone on something less than a primary relationship, like Doug and Janice. There was also the time factor to be considered. I knew John and Barbara expected us to have the whole thing reconciled by the time they returned.

I began to see the situation as totally impossible. Somebody was going to have to leave. I knew I wouldn't be able to handle it if Nanci decided to have a relationship with someone else. It had been no problem watching her and John on the living room floor, then going downstairs to fuck, Marty had fucked her before I did, but someone outside the family would just be too much.

Now it was me having trouble being with her. I wanted, and needed, to touch her, hold her, love her and feel her love in return. My love (desire?) made me want to scream the answers to her, but I couldn't. She had to reach that awareness herself, or at least ask for help. I finally decided the first thing we should do was have a meeting. At least we might be able to open up some lines of communication.

The next day, Monday, I called a meeting and the four of us really went at it. Many of the resentments that had been building up over the past two weeks came out, and by the time it was over we all felt better. No instant solutions, but at last we were dealing with some of the problems.

Tuesday night we had another meeting, and all three of us told Nanci how we felt about her attitude and behavior. Doug just flat out asked her what she was still doing there. Why didn't she leave? She tried to tell us she was "working on" herself and that she wanted to help Sandstone. We all pointed out that her recent behavior was doing just the opposite. We spent many hours talking about it., but not all the talk wa about Nanci. All four of us took our lumps that night.

The following Thursday I received a phone call from Barbara informing me they'd be back Saturday or Sunday to drop off Marty and Sue. That news caught me by surprise.

She added, "By the way, are Nanci and Janice still there?"

I told her yes, they were, but we were working on the problems.

"Okay, tom, Let's get it taken care of. Right?"

Sure, just like that. My whole time schedule had just been shot down.

Friday afternoon I met Nanci out in the courtyard, and told her I wanted her to move back in the cottage and at least try to work on the relationship. She refused. I explained that there weren't too many alternatives, but she said that if it boiled down to moving back in with me or leaving, she'd leave. I tried to reason with her, and she said she'd go for a long ride and think about it.

She came back around midnight and said, "My decision is to not move back into the cottage, and the other part of it has been decided for me, so I guess I'll have to leave." I couldn't believe it! She totally twisted it around so that we were rejecting her. We talked about it, and she had all kinds of rationalizations for her decision, toward both me and Sandstone.

"Let's face it, Tom, you'd do anything I wanted. Man, I could wrap you around my little finger."

I replied, "That's obviously not true, Nanci, or you wouldn't be in the situation you're in right now."

She was very concerned about how she'd be received when she came back up. I explained the whole thing about our "value system" and the other "value system." I don't think she understood.

Saturday evening she left.

Nanci is a perfect example of what we call "Pleasure Anxiety." It's probably one of the biggest hang-ups in our society, generally speaking, and the most over-looked by most forms of therapy. I don't pretend to be a professional in this area, but we saw so many examples of this specific behavior that it became very easy to discern.

What it boils down to is a person feeling at some level they don't deserve to feel good, enjoy themselves, and be loved. We saw too many women who were non-orgasmic and in most cases like Nanci, it went straight to Pleasure Anxiety. They refused to admit to themselves they deserved an orgasm. To make matters worse, they usually blamed their sex partner. It was all his fault for not bringing her to orgasm.

Nanci was raised in a broken home where both parents were alcoholic. She had spent much of her life trying to keep her mother from killing herself on pills and booze. It had been a hell of an experience for someone that young. Her mother had died in a fire on the day of Nanci's wedding, having fallen asleep on the couch with a lit cigarette. Nanci's new husband treated her very badly, which was, of course, just what she wanted. She had to be punished for all those terrible things she had done, especially letting her mother die like that. If Nanci had stayed with her mother, instead of going out to spend some time with friends, she was sure it would never have happened.

This all sounds like a bad soap opera, but it's very real. And it's not that unique. Many people, far too many, suffer the same kind of rejection from their parents, so they try to get what the pros call "negative attention." Children find

123

out very young that they can get attention by doing bad things. Since they can't get it any other way, thy do the bad things. That's what Nanci did when she married a man her parents resented. It was a way to get even with them

This explains her insistence that I wash my face after I performed cunnilingus, her refusal to go completely nude (she practically denied the existence of her vagina), and her over-reaction to her first orgasm. She had to turn off for fear of having another. All of a sudden sex felt good and had been fulfilling. That's exactly what it was not supposed to be for her.

Nine Days

The biggest problem we faced at Sandstone on a day-to-day basis was the same one most families have to face; meeting the budget. For over three years memberships in the Retreat were our only source of income. We need somewhere in the neighborhood of $4,500 a month to meet expenses, and at $240 a member, that's a lot of memberships. That fact alone played too large a part in our membership selection process.

Some member of the family, usually Marty or me, would conduct a short interview with the prospective members and give them a tour of the house and grounds. It was during this interview that we could try to determine their acceptability for membership based on their motivation and general behavior. By asking a few simple questions, and listening to questions being asked of us, we could pretty well determine what they were looking for. Obviously, the procedure was far from perfect, but it was relatively successful. The only real way of determining many things about these people was to watch them in an actual party environment, which was why we usually offered to let them attend one free party before they made their decision.

The conflict would start when we had too few memberships during a period, and we had someone standing in front of us with checkbook out, ready to join. We knew that the person's basic reason for joining didn't really agree with our basic philosophy, but we also knew that expenses had to be met.

In all fairness, I must say that some of the 'borderline' members went through some pretty heavy changes, and became close friends and good members. Unfortunately, others lived up to our expectations, and their memberships had to be cancelled.

I remember one man who's membership lasted all of four hours. It was a warm weekday and Marty had signed him up, getting a check for the $240. I paid little attention to the guy until another member came to me and complained, "Hey, Tom, who is that guy?" His voice indicated his displeasure.

"I don't really know, Bill. Is something wrong?"

"Yeah. He sure was bugging my wife. I finally had to tell him to leave her alone."

"Well, he's new here so let's give him a chance. I'll keep an eye on him."

It turned out I didn't have a chance to watch him. Bunny had gone from her bedroom to the adjoining bathroom and started taking a shower. The new member proceeded to walk in, take off his clothes, and climb in with her. He couldn't have picked a worse person to lay his trip on. Bunny told him in no uncertain terms to go find your own water. It got worse as the evening progressed, and his membership had to be cancelled.

We were constantly looking for way to broaden the financial base of the Foundation so the Retreat wouldn't be the only money-making aspect. Finally, in early 1972, we started branching out. First came the film company, Felidae Films, which we all felt would supply additional income to the Foundation through the production of the full-length feature motion picture about Sandstone. Then came Nexus Publications, which was going to publish a magazine and possibly some books dealing with alternative lifestyles. Finally, came the Institute, or more formally, The Institute for the Scientific Study of Sexual and Life Energy Potential. Rather all inclusive.

The idea of the Institute was to have "Experiences" similar to those taking place at the many Growth Centers around the country, but within the framework of the Sandstone philosophy. This meant including the concepts of casual nudity and open sexuality. The primary goal of the Institute, and the Retreat, was to assist people in making an emotional transition that would allow them to start considering the possibilities of Community.

Many different forms of therapy were planned, but this would take them a step further than they'd ever been before. We knew how revolutionary the concept was in the field of human behavior, and that it could have a tremendous effect on the professional community. We also knew that many of our club members were having difficulty making the transition to the concept of community, and felt this was one way of facilitating that transition.

Initially, we had a little trouble finding a Director for the operation, but finally settled on Dr. Ralph Yaney, a psychoanalyst, and his assistant, Lucille Clagett. They were both involved in private practices in the Los Angeles area, and had been 'honorary' members of Sandstone for quite a while. There were some misgivings about the choice, but we needed someone with a good professional standing to give the project the necessary legitimacy. We also wanted someone who was fully aware of our philosophy.

The Institute's first event was going to be a nine-day living experience. 16 people would come and live at the Ranch from a Friday to the following Sunday. Ideally, we hoped to have the 16 people broken down into five pair-bonds and six singles – three of each gender. We discovered very early in the interviewing stage that this breakdown was far too ideal. One of the biggest problems was finding couples who could break away from their normal lives for that long a period; what to do about their jobs, the kids, and so on. We also wanted the majority of the people to be members of Sandstone.

This was discussed with Ralph and Lucy during informal conversations, and even at a couple of Monday night meetings. We thought we had the basic operational features pretty well under control. The first inkling I had of what was really happening was when a woman came up to me during a Wednesday night party.

"Tom, what's the 9-day group thing I've been hearing about"

I explained, "We're planning on about 16 people come up here and live as a community, and give them a chance to experience what it's like. Why?"

"Well, Ralph approached me downstairs with the suggestion that I sign up for it. I told him I didn't think I could afford it, but he said that wouldn't be a problem. He'd get some guy to pay my way."

I was not happy with Ralph's method of getting members, but I gave her a brochure about the event, and told her she'd have to make up her own mind about taking part in it.

When the final choices were made, the group numbered 13. There was only one pair bond, another couple who had broken up a few days earlier, and one person who had not experienced Sandstone on a party level. One woman dropped out the first night, which left 12 – including an in-group psychologist and me. Since this was taking place while most of the family were on vacation, leaving Doug, Janice, Nanci and me to run the place, and since Nanci and I were having problems, we decided I should drop out also. The number decreased even further when one of the men became ill shortly after the start, and had to be taken to the hospital. This left the group with four males and six females.

The group was supposed to have gone through a psychological screening process, but because they were members of the Retreat, this had been neglected. A further complicating factor turned out to be that none of the group had any previous experience with the community lifestyle – including Ralph and Lucy. Although their professional standing was very high, their lack of community experience turned out to be quite a problem (as residents of the Ranch, we did live a community lifestyle).

I was fairly confident that there would be little drain on the energies of the four of us left at Sandstone, because it had been agreed that the participants in the experience would not use the main house for anything except emergencies, using the phone, or getting supplies for their kitchen. This decision was made at a Monday night meeting after much discussion. We felt that the four of us would have more than enough to do keeping the Retreat operating, and Ralph and Lucy had made it clear that they wanted the group to experience the concept of community without any help from the outside. They felt the experience would be more beneficial if they worked out their own problems.

The first participants started arriving Friday about 3:00 and we sent them directly to the North house which was going to be their home for the duration of the experience. Granted, the North house was a little small for this size group, but it was the best we could do under the circumstances. Some of the participants who were members of the Retreat came back down to the main house, but we didn't say anything, knowing that it would be taken care of that evening at the opening talk session.

Just after supper, someone came down from the North house and asked if I would come up for the talk. Doug came with me, and we sat and listened first to Ralph and then to Lucy telling the assembled group what they could expect for the next nine days. Doug gave them some general information about food, and trash disposal. I kept waiting for Ralph to tell them the ground rules as far as the main house was concerned, but he said nothing.

Ralph concluded with, "That's about all I have to say. Tom, do you have anything to add?"

Well, yeah, Ralph, there is one thing you forgot to mention. About the main house." I was beginning to feel very strange. It dawned on me that I was about to become the villain in the whole thing.

Ralph interjected that I was the representative of Sandstone in the Williamson's absence. Everyone was look at me now, waiting to hear what I had to say. Well…here goes.

"We feel that it would be best for all of us if the members of this group refrain from coming down to the main house except in cases of emergency, to use the phone, or get something out of the kitchen."

"What?"

"That's not right!"

"What's this, Tom, another one of your power trips?"

I tried to explain. "Hey look, gang, I'm just as upset as you are. In fact, I'm panicked, but for a different reason. This was all worked out and agreed to long before tonight. These aren't my instructions. This is what was decided by all of us before some went on vacation." I felt a knife twisting in my back, and I didn't like it.

One woman said, "Well, to hell with that. I don't even want to stay here if that's the way it's going to be."

Ralph said, "Now wait a minute. Why don't we take a little break, and Tom and I will talk about this. You guys just get your stuff located, and we'll be back soon." Then he turned to me. "Let's go down to the house and talk."

Ralph, Lucy, Doug, and myself returned to the main house and sat down in the living room.

I opened the conversation. "Ralph, I don't understand you. This was agreed upon by all of us a long time ago. Why didn't you say something?" I was visibly shaking. This whole thing was changing proportions faster than I could keep up with. I hadn't planned on any administrative functions; that was supposed to be taken care of by the two therapists.

"Well, Tom, I didn't want to lay that kind of restriction on them. I felt it would be better to say that we 'prefer' that they stay away from the main house. Not that they had to."

"Then why didn't you even say that much?" I was getting more upset.

Then Lucy interjected, "What difference does it make if they come down here to fuck?"

I looked at her in disbelief. "Lucy, I don't care where they do their fucking, as long as it's not on the front lawn in daytime. That's not what I'm talking about, and if you're any kind of a therapist you should know that."

Ralph asked, "Then what are you talking about, Tom?"

128

I was getting pissed. "The same thing we talked about weeks ago! Do I have to go over it again?"

"You don't have to shout. What are you talking about?"

I took a few seconds to calm down before answering quietly, "Look, that group is going to be living in an extremely emotional environment for the next nine days. If it works the way it's supposed to work, they're going to go through some pretty heavy shit. Any contact with people outside the group is going to dilute the situation. The four of us living here are also going through some heavy shit of our own; we've got the club to run, the buildings and grounds to maintain, and we don't need them coming into our space."

"Well," Lucy replied, "I still don't see what you have against them coming down here to fuck."

"I can see that I'm not getting through to you, so let's just leave it the way we planned. What I said, stands. Naturally, I'll take full responsibility for it."

That's the way it started, and it didn't improve with time.

I found out later that the one girl did drop out of the group. She had apparently made an arrangement with Ralph and Lucy that if she joined the group, she could still come down to the main house and screw her boyfriend when he came up. I never did figure out why they couldn't do their sex at the North house.

I had no contact with the group the second day until early evening when one of them came down and asked if I'd come up for a rap session. I told the other three where I'd be and left.

As soon as I entered the North House, one of the women started hovering over me, trying to get me into a conversation, or have contact with me in some manner. I finally told her with a smile, "Lynn, if you don't stop bugging me for attention, I'm going to give you some." I don't think either of us knew exactly what I meant, but it got her off my back for a while.

The rap session started out very amicably, but soon turned into an encounter. It seems they'd been talking among themselves, and had a few questions for me.

"Tom, we'd like to get to know you better. You seem to always have your defenses up, and it's difficult to get through them and find out who you really are." This from a guy who had never been to a club function.

"Well, that's easy to explain, Marv. You don't know me better simply because I don't want you to know me better."

"What?"

129

"As far as this group is concerned, Marv, I'd like to get to know him, her, and her better" (pointing at 3 people). And I'd like them to know more about me. But as far as you're concerned, and the rest of you, at this time I'm not interested in you knowing me better."

"That's not fair."

"Why not?" I asked, sensing that here was someone who didn't like rejection.

"Because I want to know you better, that's why."

"But that doesn't matter. I don't want you to know me any better. I don't know if I can trust you with any more of me than you already know, so I can't open up to you."

"That's still not fair." He was angry.

"Let me put it this way. We all start off new relationships asking ourselves, 'How much of Me can I trust him or her with?' I don't sense that I can trust you with more of me. I don't know you well enough yet."

I excused myself and went back to the Main House where there was a Saturday night party in progress. Doug and Janice were glad to see me. No sign of Nanci.

Late in the afternoon on the 4th day, I was sitting in the living talking to Janice (she's always a visual delight!) when Doug came in with a disgusted expression. "What's up?"

"Tom, what's with that group? I asked for a grocery list yesterday so I could shop for them this morning. They still can't decide what they want. I mean, what's it take to make up a grocery list?"

"Well, Doug, they're new at this, and they do need a Consensus, so don't be too hard on them."

"And where are Ralph and Lucy? I thought they were supposed to be supervising this thing. They're hardly ever around."

"Yeah, I know. I said something to Ralph about it and he just looked at me."

"Everything seems to be okay so far," Janice said. "So that means Ralph and Lucy know what they're doing. Right?"

Doug looked at her a few seconds before replying, "I sure hope so."

The following night, Tuesday, was quiet, so I went over to the cottage about 11:00 to go to bed. Nanci was still sleeping in the main house, and would hardly talk to me unless the others were there. We'd had a pretty good encounter of our own the last couple of days, and I think it helped.

I had just gotten to sleep when I heard a gawdawful, blood-curdling scream. First thing I thought of was Nanci, an intruder in the main house. I leaped out of bed, and without bothering to get dressed, took off for the main house. Just as I got in front of the swimming pool building, there was another scream. This one stopped me in my tracks, because it wasn't coming from the main house – it was coming from the North house. Then it was joined by another scream, then another and another. Must have been six people screaming. Then it stopped, and a woman laughingly said, "Far out! We'll have to do that again."

I had taken part in a couple "Games" with the group over the weekend, but those had been with Ralph and Lucy present Now it looked like they were going to play without them. They tried two different Games dealing with private space. The first was played this way; one member of the group would stand in the middle of the room and be the Passive Receiver. Then each of the other players would embrace the passive one – who wasn't supposed to respond in any way. Ralph and Lucy timed each embrace to see how long it lasted. I never did find out what it was supposed to measure, but the women got much longer embraces from both the men and the women.

The second game consisted of one player standing against the wall with a tape measure stretched out in front of them. Then each person would walk toward that person until they got as close as they felt was comfortable. Ralph and Lucy recorded the distances of each person. That one was interesting because you got a good estimate of your private space. There was one woman that I walked toward, and when I finally stopped, they couldn't measure the distance between us with a micrometer!

The sixth day, Wednesday, dawned absolutely beautiful! It couldn't have been better if the Chamber of Commerce ordered it. I was out of bed at 9:00, and walked over to the office to get some papers. As I passed the North House one of the women was getting in her car. I said "Good morning!" and really meant it. She said the same thing back at me, she was going down the hill to check on her kids or buy groceries. I can't remember exactly, because I was distracted. She was not modest getting in the car and she was Commando. I found the papers in the office and was on my way back to the cottage. I only stayed there a few minutes before deciding it was time for my first cup of coffee, so I headed for the Main House. I was just outside the swimming pool when I heard the female scream.

"Help! Help!" It came from far away. "Somebody help me!"

131

At first, I couldn't tell where it was coming from. Sound can be very deceptive in the mountains. But after hearing it repeated, I pin-pointed it on the upper road. Nanci was coming out on the front porch, and she heard it also.

"Call the cops, Nanci!" Without asking a question, she went back inside. I ran back to the cottage and grabbed a pair of shorts, then ran over to the Jeep. I drove up the road still hearing that mournful call for help.

A short distance up the road, I saw a small, blood-splattered girl trying to walk toward me, but have a great deal o difficulty. She was wearing a very thin, short dress that was almost ripped off her. It wasn't until I stopped the Jeep and got out that I recognized her as the woman I'd seen earlier.

She almost collapsed in my arms when I got to her, so I picked her up and carried her over to the Jeep. Then I raced back down to the Main House where Nanci and Janice were waiting. I carried her into the bedroom and put her on the big bed. It was obvious she was in a state of shock. She just kept crying and moaning and begging us to help her. We could see she wasn't hurt too badly on the surface, but we had no idea about inside. Her body was covered with scrapes and burns. There wasn't a lot of blood, just a little coming from numerous places. She just kept begging us to help her. "Please, Tom. I promise I won't try to hurt myself again!"

Flashback! That was exactly the same thing Pamela had said when they pumped out her stomach. We tried to quiet her, but she wouldn't stop promising us that she really wasn't trying to kill herself, and she'd never do it again. All we could get out of her was that she'd jumped out of the car while it was moving, and just let it go.

The Highway Patrol got there almost the same time as the ambulance, and the officer told me he'd stopped to check the car, and it was okay. I went up later and found it of the road in a ditch. It would take a tow truck to get it out.

I called Ralph and told him what happened and her condition. He actually sounded very irritated that his schedule was being interrupted by this! He asked if we could bring her down to his office (what for???), but I told him the ambulance was taking her to the hospital.

The whole group was supposed to attend the Wednesday night party, but I thought it was a bad idea. The Wednesday night parties are low-key, usually when we invite potential members up. I didn't like where the group's collective head was at, and didn't like putting them in contact with the unsuspecting club members. But they came to the party.

Everything went well that night. The group members finally decided the club members were boring and the party was dull. They left early to have their own party in the North House.

The woman who had the accident returned to the group on Thursday, the seventh day, against my wishes, and got what she wanted – attention. She was the female half of the only pair bond in the group, and her mate had gotten turned on by some o the other women. Since there were no men in the group she really liked, she felt cheated, and wanted him to spend more time with her (Time Jealousy!). After her freakout, he and the rest of the group gave her what she wanted.

The in-group psychologist, who went through some pretty heavy changes herself, took the injured woman under her wing, and spent most o her time listening to the woman's complaints about her current relationship. When I visited the North House, just the two of them were there. All the rest had gone down the hill.

The injured woman was lying on the mattress, obviously still stiff and sore from her experience, and the psychologist was sitting next to her with a plastic cup of yogurt and some graham crackers. They talked to me in strange, far away voices, and the psychologist was trying to spread yogurt on the crackers and eat them the whole time I was there. Most of the yogurt never got to the crackers, most of it ended up on the floor and on her. She seemed completely unconscious of what she was doing with her hands.

I could make very little sense out of what they were saying, and there didn't seem to be anything else I could do, so I returned to my own form of insanity at the Main house. That was about the last time I visited the North House. Four of the group who had gone down the hill called me later and said they weren't coming back until the following evening, so the last days o the Experience were like a decompression for most o the group. They did come to our Saturday night party, but once again decided it was too tame for them and left early.

I understand that Dr. Yaney is planning to write a paper about the Experience, and I would be very interested in reading it. I don't feel the group learned very much about Community living. Doug and I talked about it later, and agreed the group had trouble from the beginning with simple things like buying food and waste disposal. We found quite a bit of trash hidden in the cupboards when we visited the house after they left. All I know about the Experience is that three people changed their names. What's that mean?

They Get Harder

John and Barbara and Marty and Sue came back yesterday afternoon, no more than an hour after Nanci left. The first thing they asked me was about Nanci. I told them she had just left. They also asked about Janice, and I told them they might be a little surprised by Janice. She was going through some very good changes, and I could see no justification for asking her to leave also.

"Good!" was Barbara's comment. "I'm glad that's finally straightened out."

"How'd the trip go, Barb?"

"Well, there wasn't too much conversation, but there was a lot of communication."

Sue disagreed, but then I guess she didn't understand the difference. John said they drove almost to the Yukon, couldn't find a place to park, so drove home. Sue brought a roaring toothache home, which didn't help the general vibes at all. Barbara also said Sue was on a giant ego trip, and that both Marty and Sue are having trouble, individually and in the relationship. Personally, I'm not getting good vibes from them, but part of that could be because of Sue's tooth ache.

Barbara and I were out on the front porch. "So how'd it go, Tom?"

"It was hell. I've never been through such an ordeal and don't plan on doing it again."

"Yeah, I know what you mean. I went through some pretty heavy shit myself the last few days. Sometimes I just wanted to grab Sue by that long, blonde hair, and toss her around the motor home. But it wouldn't have helped, she just doesn't understand."

"That's exactly how I felt about Nanci. I just wanted to scream at her. But, like you said, it wouldn't have done any good."

"It was a growing experience for both of us, Tom."

"That it was, Barb."

"Well, I can give you one piece of advice."

"What's that?"

"They get harder."

"Oh, thanks! That's just what I need to hear." We both laughed, but we knew we'd both grown from the experiences.

134

John and I finally had a chance to sit down and talk about Nexus Magazine. I told him about the articles we'd received, probably enough for two issues.

"That's great, Tom. Do you think you could publish a Magazine and travel around the country at the same time?"

"I don't know what you mean, John."

"Well, I was thinking of selling the Ranch, buying some good vehicles and traveling for about a year. We'd be finding out what's happening around the country, and look for the right spot to start the large-scale community."

"Sounds great, John. I'm sure we could do it as long as I had someone in one spot who could coordinate the whole thing."

"Okay, let's start thinking along those lines. Barb and I are going to take off again for a few days, so take care of things while we're gone. We'll call you later."

Maybe this is just what I need to get Nanci back. She would welcome an opportunity like this; lots of travel, meeting interesting people, fantastic education. I called her and made a date for her to come back up the following Tuesday. When she got there, I told her our plans, and she replied that she had some good news of her own. Her father had asked her to move back in with him and offered to pay her way through college. Obviously, his was the better offer, and she was truly happy with it. Unfortunately, it never happened. We found out later that he'd backed out on the plan, and left her out in the cold. She paid one more visit to the Ranch, and it looked like she sincerely wanted to stay, but she just couldn't bring herself to ask. That was the last contact I had with her.

Soon after John and Barbara left, Doug decided to take his vacation also. After he was gone over two weeks without even a phone call, we all started worrying. We didn't know where he was going or how long he planned on staying, but we knew he didn't have a car and was probably hitch-hiking. We all agreed that was not the safest way to travel.

He showed up on Monday morning, wondering what we were all so worried about, and a little pleased that we were. He told us he'd been to San Francisco, then flew to Hawaii. That was quite a vacation! When he arrived at the airport the night before, it was after midnight – not a good time to be hitch-hiking. So he called the Ranch. It took a while to wake anybody, but Marty finally answered the phone. Doug told him where he was, and asked if he or somebody else, could come and get him. Marty refused.

That shook the whole community quite a bit. It was understood by most of us that if a member asked for help, it was our responsibility to respond. Where was Marty's head? We knew he'd been having trouble lately, but this was outrageous. A couple of times he came out of the bedroom in the morning and jumped on the first person he came in contact with. Bunny and I had been two of his targets, she for letting the cats in the house, me for letting someone watch their TV while they were gone; both very minor incidents that he used to project his own problems on us.

There was a time after Nanci left when I went on a sexual rampage. The last couple of weeks before she left, I discovered I was almost totally impotent, and after she left I felt a tremendous need to reaffirm my masculinity. I tried once in the pool with a woman Gay had invited down from San Francisco. I did get an erection, but couldn't orgasm.

Nanci had walked by the pool door while that was happening, but I never found out what she thought of the scene. When the woman and I finally gave up, we returned to the Main house. We sat down on the couch, an she reached for her purse to get a cigarette. As she put the pack back in her purse, she lifted a wallet out of a side pocket and opened it to reveal a badge. I'd screwed a cop! Actually, she was an employee of the California State Corrections institute, working with delinquents. But she still had that badge.

Late in August, I regained my manhood, and I did it in grand fashion. The quality wasn't the best I ever had, but the quantity was certainly there. And not just on party nights, I was busy during the day and on quiet week nights.

I remember one Tuesday night I was out on the terrace with two women. I'd already had sex with one of them that afternoon, and now I had an arm around each of them, kissing and feeling one woman while the other was masturbating with a portable vibrator. Even for this place, that was outrageous.

Then the woman I'd screwed that afternoon, Lynn, got turned on to the other woman, Kathy, who had never had same-sex contact before, so she started clinging to me. That got Lynn upset, so the three of us went over to my cottage and talked about it. I ended up screwing Kathy with Lynn beside us. I tried to pull Lynn in with us, but she wanted Kathy all to herself.

Kathy stayed at the cottage until Friday. She was into a very heavy fusion trip, and refused to read my signals or even listen to my words (except the ones she wanted to hear). So I finally had to make it very clear that she was leaving me no alternative but to reject her completely. She refused to lighten up. It had to be all or nothing. I picked nothing. We parted friends, and I assured her she was welcome to visit anytime as my guest, but we were not going to have a Primary Relationship.

A few weeks later, she jumped at the chance to drive me up to Oregon for my nephew's wedding. When we'd been on the empty freeway a while, she unzipped her jeans, pushed them and her underwear down below her knees, and spread her legs so I could play with her to relieve the boredom. When I touched her, I was surprised to find she was already wet. So I parted her labia with my fingers, then began caressing her vulva. I had no trouble finding her swollen clitoris, and it didn't take much coaxing before she had an orgasm. She pulled her clothes back up and relaxed.

About a half-hour later she admitted she faked the orgasm. I told her it didn't feel just right, and told myself I couldn't trust her.

Wednesday night I signed in about 56 people for the party, and after checking out all the women, I turned to Barbara and said, "Congratulations! You're the only woman here. All the rest are just little girls." Naturally, she agreed with me.

It was almost one month after Nanci let that I met Kris. Bunny and I were downstairs talking, and I was aware of a woman behind us kept looking at me. Her partner had already fallen asleep.

Suddenly, the side door opened and a guy walked in. Bunny and I looked at him, then at each other and smiled. Yep. He was a gate-crasher. I waited until he was in the middle of the room before I approached him. "Hi, my name is Tom, I'm kind of the Manager here, and I don't remember signing you in.

He was nervous. "Oh, well…I don't think you did. Must have been someone else."

"But someone did sign you in?"

"Oh, sure. Long ago."

"Okay," I said smiling. "Maybe we could go upstairs and check. I like to keep track of everyone here."

By now, everybody was aware of what was happening. They knew he was a gate-crasher, and wanted to see how I handled it.

I turned and headed or the stairs, making sure he was following me. Just as I took the first step up, I heard a shuffle and turned to see him running for the door. He'd come in nude, and when he ran out, I saw him turn the wrong way heading for the front lawn. Not sure he could get back to his car without getting some nicks and bruises climbing back up the hillside.

I went back over to Bunny, but she was already walking toward the door. "I'm beat, Tom, talk to you tomorrow."

"Okay, Bunny, good night." I turned and looked at the young woman on the mattress, and she was still watching me. So I went over and introduced myself, sitting down beside her.

"Does that happen often, Tom?"

"You mean that guy?"

"Yeah."

"Oh, once in a while. They usually don't stay too long. We know most of our members by sight, so it's pretty easy to spot. Having a good time?"

"Not really. I've been here all night, and I've only found one person I want to get to know."

"Really. Who is the lucky person?" I had a feeling I knew the answer.

"You, and you've been pretty busy."

"Well, I'm not busy now, so let's get acquainted."

Kris and I spent all of Sunday and part of Monday together. She was very open and straightforward about her desire to move in with me, but I put her off. I wanted to make sure it wasn't a rebound thing, or that I was just using her to see if I was ready for another relationship. I wanted to make sure of my motivation before starting something, so I sent her home Monday for a few days.

John and Barbara were leaving again for a visit to the Pacific Northwest, and I wasn't too happy to see them go. Even though they didn't help out much running the club, it was comforting to know they were there if I needed them. They were about the only two people I could talk to. Marty and Sue were spending most of their time in the bedroom, and Jon and Bunny were totally involved in the beginning stages of editing the film. The rest of the family were into their own trips.

One of the men who was helping to sync the sound on the movie asked me if I thought the movie was an honest portrayal of life at Sandstone. I thought a minute before I told him, "I think the movie is an honest picture of life at Sandstone – while a movie is being made here. Obviously, making the movie was part of the whole Gestalt, so it affected all of our behavior."

Kris's friend, Jim, brought her back up Wednesday afternoon and we spent the night together. I was really happy. In many ways, she was exactly the type of woman I was looking for, but we both held back; the fear of getting hurt again.

For one week after Kris came up, things were really good. Granted, Marty and I locked horns almost daily, but Kris kept making things for the cottage, and helped Sue and Janice with the cooking. Kris and I were getting along very nicely. It was nice to find out I wasn't afraid to love, to take risks and make myself vulnerable again.

Jim came up one afternoon to get some sun, and when he was getting ready to leave, Kris suggested that she'd go with him to get some clothes and other things at her mother's house. That sounded like a good idea. For one thing, it meant she was ready to make a commitment to me and Sandstone. It also saved me the trouble of taking her down the hill.

"I'll go with Jim, then call you this evening and tell you where to pick me up. Come to think of it, I should probably spend some time with my family since I haven't told them anything about you and this place. But either way, I'll call you tonight and tell you when to come and get me."

It was the last I ever saw of Kris.

She never called, wrote, got in touch with Jim, or anything. She just completely disappeared. I contacted her mother once, and she told me she knew where Kris was, and would tell her I tried to contact her. I concluded it had only been a Game with her until it came time to really make a commitment. I could understand it intellectually, but not emotionally. Why are so many people afraid of Love? How many times will I have to give my Love before I find someone strong enough to at least accept it, and maybe even return it?

Bunny summed it up very nicely when she said, "Well, Tom, you did everything right...and still lost."

John and Barbara made two trips to the north country by mid-September, and there was more talk about the large-scale community they were planning. It had started out as an adjunct to the existing Sandstone, and was to be located in up-state New York. That plan fell through rather quickly, and that's when they started looking at alternate sites in the Pacific Northwest. When they returned from the second trip, they were excited about some land they'd found in Montana, and the rumor was they'd already put a deposit on it. That caused quite a stir among the family members, because there was instant speculation on who would be going with them, and who would continue operating Sandstone – if

139

there was even going to be a Sandstone. None of us could see where they could get the money for an operation as big as they were discussing without selling the Ranch, and they weren't volunteering very much information. But why should they? This was all their trip, and the rest of us were just along for the ride. At least that's the way it seemed sometimes.

On September 29th, the guessing game was over – Sandstone Ranch had been sold. Or at least the deal was in escrow. It was hard to sort out all the emotions I felt about the news; some relief, more resentment. I resented John and Barbara sacrificing Sandstone for the large-scale community, partly because I didn't know much about it, and I wasn't that interested in it. I liked Sandstone just the way it was and had been for five years while I lived and worked there.

John and Barbara were going to make another trip to Montana, and asked me to go with them – I refused. Even though they seemed to be planning on me as a member of the new community, I had doubts about the whole thing.

I felt the sale of Sandstone would be a big mistake, what with all we'd been through in the last 4-1/2 years. We were finally beginning to achieve a level of acceptance and legitimacy that had been a major stumbling block in the past. We had articles in Penthouse and Esquire and even Playboy (without mentioning our name). We'd finally won the legal battle, and what a battle that was two years ago. I can remember the scene at the Welfare Commission as if it was last week.

It all started when the Los Angeles County board of Supervisors passed an ordinance requiring all "Growth Centers" to be licensed. The license cost $10.00, so this was a control mechanism, not a money-maker. We received a notice in the mail, along with an application for the license, informing us we were considered a growth center and would have to buy the license. Of course there was a hearing necessary to determine if we were entitled to it. Their definition of a "Growth Center" was interesting; something about "any place where three or more people, not of the same family, congregate and expose themselves in the nude for the purpose of recreation or therapy."

Actually, we were getting hit on a shotgun blast on the license. We never had any complaints from the neighbors, the authorities (sheriffs liked our coffee on late Saturday nights!), or anybody else, but there was another place in the same area that wasn't quite as discreet. Elysium Fields is located right in the middle of Topanga Canyon, surrounded by private homes. It's more like a real growth center because a lot of money is charged and there's a lot of talk. Nudity is allowed, and some of the members have been known to go outside the walls and bother the neighbors. That's where the complaints were coming from, but I guess they decided to "clean up" the whole area at the same time. Both us and Elysium received notices in the mail.

Elysium didn't even bother filling out the application. They immediately took the matter to court. We did fill out our application, and received a notice of when the hearing would be held.

The County Welfare Commission was the group who was going to decide if we qualified or the license. If they hand-picked the members of the Commission, they couldn't have done a better job. I don't think any of them were under 65 years old, and the sour looks we got when we walked in gave us fair-warning of what was to come. Even the audience was stacked against us. The whole room was packed with middle-age Valley housewives who looked like they wanted a lynching party.

John and Albert were the spokesmen for Sandstone, and they answered a few preliminary questions about the Retreat. At one point, one of the commissioners had to go outside and consult with his attorney before asking John about the sexual activity that went on. You could almost smell the lust in the room.

Then they brought on their "witnesses". There was a preacher from some small church down in Topanga Canyon who told an incredible story about a teen-age boy who wandered into his church. The boy told him he'd gotten lost in the fog and ended up at Sandstone asking for help. According to this preacher, the boy was stripped of his clothes and forced to take part in all kinds of immoral and illegal sex acts with different people. The ladies in the audience squirmed in their seat during all this.

John responded by simply saying, "You're a liar."

Of course, the preacher had no corroborating evidence, like producing the boy, but he did get his say.

Another witness was one of the housewives, and she made Carrie Nation look meek and mild. This lady was on a crusade to rid our country of those nasty smut peddlers and sex fiends once and for all! She came to the witness chair carrying a large suitcase. She opened it and pulled out copies of "girlie" Magazines, and even a few "beaver" Magazines. The suitcase was stuffed with them. She held them up to show the audience the contents. She explained that this was the type of thing being disseminated by us and other "perverts" in the canyon.

First of all, Sandstone Ranch is not in the canyon, it's located on a plateau on Saddle Peak Rd. atop the mountain on the west side of the canyon. The graphic display upset the commission members so much they finally insisted that she stop showing the Magazines. At that time, the only thing we were publishing was a monthly newsletter to our members, and it contained no photographs. But she also had her say.

Obviously, we were refused a license. We didn't stop operating, and we did file a lawsuit after receiving a citation for operating without a license. The whole thing was crazy, but it did get us a lot of publicity. There were stories in all the papers, and we even got on a local TV news show. They did have video of us walking around the grounds nude! Rear views only.

It took over a year, and $20,000, but we finally won the lawsuit. The ordinance was tossed out as being unconstitutional – the First Amendment.

Another financial hassle we had was raising money for the documentary motion picture. We finally did get the money and it was produced. We were getting well-known nationally and even internationally. There was a Magazine in Sweden offering a special charter flight to Sandstone. We'd done a few network TV shows, and Bob Francoeur had described our operation in his new book, *Eve's New Rib*. So many good things were finally beginning to happen!

John had always described himself as a pragmatist, but I began to feel the decision to sell the Ranch was not pragmatic. I thought a real pragmatist would see the value of holding on for another year or so: Give the movie a chance to be released, see if Mr. Talese does write about us in his book, see what kind of offers begin to pour in. We had the Institute started, and Nexus Publications was beginning to take shape. Marty had some good lectures lined up.

I remember wishing John an Barbara would just climb in their motor-home and travel. Why don't they go away for a while and let us continue running the Retreat.

A Community of Three

After the rumors that Sandstone had been sold started spreading, everyone's mood and behavior changed. Trying to sell memberships became very difficult, though still necessary because we had to eat and pay the bills. The Ranch had been in escrow before and had not made it. It didn't take long before the rumors started spreading among the members, and that made things even more difficult, because they would tell prospective members not to waste their money. I was asked if the place had been sold a number of times, and denied it – based on the fact that the sale was still in escrow.

Doug was the first to know I wasn't going with the Williamsons. I told him in the car when we were going down to buy groceries. He was a little surprised by the news and disappointed. A community of three to start. Not very big. That's what it looked like. No one else in the family expected to be asked to join them.

When we got back from the city, I decided to find out where Marty's head was at about the future. I knew he had been talking to some members about opening another Retreat, and that was what I had in mind also. We met in the living room, and Sue joined us.

"Yeah, we have plans. Let me show you the drawings we have of the physical layout of the place we're considering."

I stopped him. "Marty, I don't have to see those. I want to know more about the actual operation of the place you're thinking about."

He explained it. "Well, I want to get away from the club aspect of the whole thing, and get more into the management part. I don't feel it's necessary to have a large group living together, and I think it will help keep the overhead down if we hire people to come in and do the work as employees."

We were obviously in two completely different ball parks. "That's too bad, Marty, because I feel that the community living here acts as a role model of the lifestyle we're trying to sell. I would change some of the structure of the operation, to put it on a paying basis, but I'd never change that part."

The constant threat of not being able to pay our bills was the most destructive aspect of our present structure. It was the main reason Marty became less discriminating about accepting memberships ("If they've got the money, let 'em join – we can always cancel their memberships later without a refund"). That only helped to further our public iMage as a "fuck club."

It was interesting to watch Sue during this conversation, because her body language, nods, smiles, finger-pointing, told me she was agreeing with what I said, but couldn't say so out-loud, because that would be a threat to her relationship. She had to appear to be on Marty's side, and that bothered her because she didn't like his side.

The next few months were pretty bad for all of us, because we knew the end was near and we had to make plans for the future. Marty and Sue started conferring with Ralph Yaney about getting a new Retreat going, and I had to decide if that's what I really wanted – maybe on a smaller scale.

Nexus publications became a reality when John and Barbara and me went to the newspaper and filed a fictitious name certificate. I started working on publishing "Hot and Cool Sex" as an excerpt from Francoer's new book, smaller and with photos. Maybe that would be the thing that sustained me for the time being. If we could get that published in time, and find a distributor, it might make it pretty big.

Doug was already set to go with John and Barbara, Jonathan and Bunny were far from finishing editing the movie, and Janice and her daughter were planning on going off with Janice's boyfriend.

So we were all pretty set in our plans. At the same time, we were trying to maintain the club a while longer, but the new owners had started spreading the word that they'd bought the place. That made it almost impossible to deny the Ranch had been sold. I'd tell people it was just in escrow and that had fallen through before, but it didn't work – if it wasn't in escrow, it was sold. Some members were very upset that the Retreat was closing, because that meant they'd have to find a substitute on their own.

Some long-time members were really upset by the news, and I could empathize with them. But they were only about 10% of the membership. The rest of the members had very little idea of what we were really trying to accomplish at Sandstone, and only looked at as a place where they could go for a wild party with lots of sex. Granted, a few of them were beginning to work through their sexual fantasies, but the number was too small.

When the word got out that the sale was in escrow, people started coming out of the woodwork with plans to buy the Ranch, and continue operating the Retreat. But all of those plans turned out to be just more fantasies.

Jane

Today is all sufficient for
The things that must be done
But pleasure inevitably seems
To be more fun

Tomorrow never comes to us
As yesterday it seemed
So put your thoughts together
And do the things you dreamed

From Jane
P.S. Belated Happy Valentine's Day

Those words were written by one of the best friends and most beautiful people I knew during my time at Sandstone. As I remember it, she first came to Sandstone on a Sunday afternoon with a couple who had recently joined. I first saw them downstairs and they introduced her to me. She was wearing a long, brightly printed dress with some kind of Indian design, and that, plus her very long straight black hair and full lips, gave me the impression that she was Indian. It turned out later that she wasn't. She didn't appeal to me physically at first, but she turned out to be a very special individual in many other ways.

We did eventually have a physical relationship, but it was more an extension of our deep friendship than just a joining of two people. When I think of the three reasons why people should have sexual relations, I know that it certainly wasn't blocking my relationship with Jane. Yes, we probably did know each other more fully after doing it, but it only deepened our love. The third reason, because it's fun and it feels good, is probably the most appropriate reason we made love.

I watched her have sexual relations with other men at the parties, but it never bothered me or lessened the depth of my love. She had the same physical needs as the rest of us, and it wasn't difficult to see that she felt very differently with them than she did with me.

She came upstairs one Saturday night and sat down next to me on a couch. She looked a little distraught, and nervously lit a cigarette before she spoke. "I've got a good idea, Tom/"

"What's that?"

"I think you should put a big sign on the wall downstairs."

I smiled, "And what should the sign say, love?"

"It should say, 'IF YOU HAVE TO ASK, FORGET IT.'"

I had to think about that for a minute, but when I finally got it, I started laughing. "Wow! That's beautiful!" She was beginning to see the humor in it and started laughing softly. "Do you really think it would help?"

She stopped laughing. "Hell, I don't know. Some of those guys don't listen to a word I say. God, they're gross!"

"Hey, if somebody is getting pushy, I want to know about it, Jane. You know that's not allowed. You want me to go back downstairs with you?" Sometimes the mere presence of a family member in the party environment changes people's behavior.

"I don't think it would help, sweet. I think they want to be gross." She was obviously not happy tonight.

"Let me explain something about male behavior. Maybe it will help you understand."

"What's that?" She didn't seem interested.

"Well there are some guys, and a few ladies, who come to the parties and only approach the people they're sure will reject them."

"What? You're kidding!" I had her attention, now.

"No, I'm not. They seem to have excellent radar working. They can tell from clear across the room if a person will reject them, and they only approach the ones they feel sure about. If they're radar is off a little, they will get gross just to make sure you reject them."

"Why the hell would they do that?"

"I assume they're more afraid of acceptance than rejection. Acceptance would mean they'd have to perform, and that can be scary as hell for a man. That's why it's much more predominant in men than women."

She laughed, "Yeah, we don't have to worry about getting it up. That would make a difference."

"Right. If this was a normal cocktail party, the big fear would probably be rejection. But up here it's just the opposite for a lot of guys. Everything is so up

146

front here, the nudity, and the open environment, without all the games, they can't even engage in polite conversation for fear it will escalate."

She thought about it for a minute, then said, "So they pick a woman they're sure will say no, then they start hitting on her, knowing all the time that they're safe, and telling themselves it's her fault for refusing me. Wow, that is so weird. How do you handle it?"

"Well, usually I don't have to. That's more in your area of expertise. The only time I get involved is if the guy gets really obnoxious and a member tells me about him. Then I have a little talk with him."

She leaned over and kissed me. "Thanks, Tom. That was very important."

Jane helped me out a number of times, always there when I needed her, but the time I remember best is when they were filming the party. Jon and Bunny had planned that as the culmination of their shooting schedule.

The preparation for filming the party was intense. There were extra lights and microphones, testing and adjusting, both in the main house and outside. A few extra people had to be hired, and the whole crew were briefed a number of times.

The party was planned for a Friday night, and it looked like we might have as many as seventy or eighty people attending. As usual, there was no planned activity at the party, although we did entice the members by offering a full-course buffet dinner. We hoped that everything would happen spontaneously like it did at every party. The only difference would be the lights, camera and microphones. The lights were the most inhibiting.

The week leading up to the party was not a happy one. A lot of bad things happened in a short period of time. John had to shoot a wild dog, the reflecting pool in front of the main house started leaking and had to be drained. Many of the fish in the pool died during the procedure, and John and Barbara's pet bobcat, P.C., ran away. On a more personal note, Nanci was refusing to speak to me. So none of the family were in a good mood that Friday, but realized the importance of this party, and we seemed to draw energy from each other – it's called Synergy.

By the time the club members started arriving, we were all in a good mood, and the atmosphere was warm and friendly. My main problem was Nanci – she refused to have anything to do with me, but seemed to brighten up when a camera was pointed at her. And then Jane walked in.

My greeting was so warm, and the hugs and kisses lasted so long, she was caught a little off guard.

"Wow! That's some greeting."

"Jane, you have no idea how glad I am to see you. Are you alone?"

"Yes. Is that okay?"

"It's perfect."

"Why? What's up?"

"My love, I have a little problem, and need your help."

"Okay. What can I do?"

I explained the situation with Nanci and how important this party was to all of us. I asked her if she'd consider herself my date for the evening.

"Hell yes, Tom," she murmured in a very seductive voice. Then with a wink and a wiggle, added, "What are friends for?"

We both laughed and embraced. It was the first of many embraces that night, one of them even made it on film. Try making love with a camera eight inches from your ear!

The Feline Family

When I first visited Sandstone, there was only one feline living there – Pusso. He was a large, beautiful, all-black Manx cat – with an attitude. He looked and acted like he owned the place, and it was not a good idea to argue the point with him. At times he could be affectionate, like when he'd jump up in your lap and start sucking your fingers one at a time. But if you walked by him and failed to give him proper recognition, he might grab you around the ankle (with all claws out) and hold on until you gave him what he considered the proper amount of attention.

I walked in the front door one Monday night to attend the meeting, and found Mag and Pusso laying on the floor, their faces only inches away from each other. I said, "Hi," and was shushed by Mag. "We're having a conversation."

Pusso had left the Ranch by the time I moved in, but there were others to replace him. First, there was the original P.C. (Pussy Cat) who Mag found living in a storm drain. She spent many hours talking to that cat before it would come out. It was months before P.C. would have anything to do with people, except Mag.

At one point, there were as many as fourteen cats living at the Ranch. They had names like Mouse, Jasper, Gypsy, Ashley, Chin, Professor, A.C. (Another cat) and D.C. (Da last cat). Some of them didn't last too long because of the predators living in the mountains – like packs of wild dogs.

The only non-feline member of our animal family was Jenny, the mule. Michael had brought her up as a present for Janice. Jenny didn't last too long either – she strangled herself on her own rope.

The only other feline member of the family I haven't mentioned was Big P.C. Actually, his full name was P.C. Felidae.

P.C. was a beautiful, young, Canadian bobcat the Williamsons had obtained from a zoo in South Dakota in December of 1971 while on one of their trips. They were living in the motor home, and P.C. became the third member of a very unique triad. Since he lived here, the only time the rest of us saw him was when they would bring him down to the main house in the VW and let him sit outside.

When they first brought him into the house, we all thought he was a very pretty kitty-cat. But as he grew older, we all gained a great deal of respect, and some fear. He was, without a doubt, the most valid feedback we could get on where we were psychologically.

P.C. decided that the most interesting thing he could do on his infrequent trips to the main house was to test us. How does a bobcat test you? Well, he might just sit down in front of you and stare. Now, having a bobcat stare at me is not my idea of a great way to start the day, and since they usually brought him down in the morning, that's when the testing occurred.

Not only would he sit and stare at you, but after a few minutes of that, realizing he wasn't having the desired effect, he would raise his butt off the carpet and start wiggling it back and forth. Now I don't care if it's a bobcat or just a little pussy cat, when they do that, it means they're getting ready to pounce. How would you feel knowing a bobcat is getting ready to pounce on you? Well, we found out because he would pounce. Actually, he didn't jump on us as much as over us. He would kind of run up the front of you, then jump over the back of the couch. As long as you did nothing more than cover your eyes, you were safe. Unless he sensed that you were really afraid of him. Then he could drive you out of the house just by lying on the back of the couch and staring at your ear – as he did with Gay Talese.

One of his favorite games was to hide behind the couch and jump out at you when you came from the kitchen. He did that to me once when I had a cup of coffee in hand. Only he didn't jump past me, he jumped on my leg. All four paws on my naked thighs! Fortunately, he kept his claws in, but the force of his jump did spill some coffee. Once he hit the floor, he turned to see what my reaction to his attack was. Without giving me a chance to recover, he jumped a second time. Only this time, he put three paws on me and too a wild swing at the coffee cup with the fourth paw. If he hadn't knocked me back a couple of inches, he would have had coffee all over him and the carpet. John chased him away before he tried Strike Three.

He played that game with me a number of times in the morning, but it got a little boring; we both knew what we were going to do. So to liven things up a bit, I decided to play a trick on him. When he saw me head for the kitchen with my coffee cup, he dodged behind the couch. When I came back, I walked especially heavy. Just as I got to a spot about a foot from where I knew he liked to jump, I stopped walking, but paced in place. He fell for it. He leaped out a good two feet in front of me. When he landed without hitting anything, he turned around and gave me a look that could kill, then walked away from me while I was laughing. I knew it was only a temporary victory; you don't laugh at a bobcat without expecting some repercussions.

He got his chance a couple of nights later. It was quiet, nobody had come up, so John brought P.C. in the house. The phone rang and I answered it; some guy wanted information on the club. I started giving him the tape-recorded type answers I usually give, when all of a sudden I had a twenty-pound bobcat sitting on my head with all four paws in my face!

"Hey, uh, I'm sorry, but I've got a bobcat sitting on my head."

"A what?"

"Never mind. Could you call back tomorrow, please?"

"I guess so. What's on your head?"

"Good night." Of course P.C. jumped off as soon as I hung up the phone.

When I was going through any emotional problems, I couldn't go over to the main house too early, because P.C. would sense it, and just not leave me alone. The last thing I needed was a bobcat psyching me out.

He seemed to have a special thing for the female members of the family, and I'd say he managed to freak out every one of them, with the exception of Bunny. He was playing with her one night and, almost by accident, sank his teeth into her arm. As soon as he did it, he knew he'd screwed up. He looked at her and John with a very embarrassed expression in his eyes, but couldn't let go. John finally had to pry his jaws apart. Ever since that incident, he and Bunny have gotten along quite well.

Bunny wasn't the only person he bit, just the first. He also bit Janice, but that's because he sensed her fear. After that, she refused to come in the house if he was there, which was the smartest way to handle it. I know John says you have to work through your fears, but trying to work through that one could have caused Janice a lot of pain.

We were all curious about what P.C. would do to the other cats around the Ranch, and he showed us. P.C. loved to play in the large fishpond in front of the house (he also liked the swimming pool; he would lean over and smack the water with his paw). We just had one cat at the time, jasper, who was a real city slicker type cat; he'd strut around totally fearless. He just happened to be on the porch one morning when John arrived with P.C., and stopped strutting long enough to check out the big dude. Before Jasper had time to run, P.C. had him in the pool and bouncing his head off the bottom a half dozen times before Jasper was able to get out from under that paw. He came out of the water with every hair sticking straight out – even though he was soaking wet.

P.C. spent a lot of time in the VW bug parked in the courtyard in front of the main house. John let the windows down a few inches for air, and when P.C. got tired of chewing the door and window knobs, he'd hide on the floor and wait for some unsuspecting individual to walk by within reach. Then he'd come off the floor like a bullet, stick his paw out and smack the hapless passerby. One night he did it to a member headed up to the pool, but instead of just slapping her, he grabbed her towel and took it in the car. John had to go out and talk him into giving it back.

If John and Barbara forgot to feed P.C. on time, he usually took their bedclothes off the bed and crapped on the mattress. The last few months we were open, it was difficult for any of us to tolerate P.C.'s games – we were all on edge and he sensed it. So it got to the point where John and Barbara had the house to themselves in the morning. We finally brought it up at a Monday night meeting. They didn't agree, of course, they thought it was our problem. But we didn't see P.C. in the morning as often.

The friendliest thing P.C. could do was turn around and present his testicles to a person. To be allowed to rub a bobcat's balls was definitely an act of faith.

151

Unfortunately, the few people he did present his testicles to had no idea what he wanted, and were afraid he'd defecate on them.

It was during the last week of filming that P.C. ran away. It was a pure case of growing up, just like a lot of teens, he had to express his independence. Since everything else went wrong that week, it fit right in. John and Barbara didn't hold out much hope for his return. There are other bobcats running wild around Sandstone, so it was assumed P.C. would find a mate and set up housekeeping. But the Friday night we were filming the party, a girl walked in the front door and told me there was a "very big kitty" in the middle of our pond. P.C. was back! As much hassle as we had with that damn cat, I don't think there was anybody who wasn't happy about his return. He was part of our family.

Judith

I was greeting members and guests for another Saturday night brain-frying party at Sandstone when an attractive couple walked in the front door. I prided myself on knowing all the members by face and most by name. This couple were not members.

"Hi, I'm Tom. Welcome to Sandstone."

The man held out his hand and I shook it. "Hi, Tom. I'm John Bullero and this is my wife, Judith."

"Hi, John," I replied, "Are you here as guests of...excuse me. Did you say John and Judith Bullero???" Lights in my head were flashing.

"That's right."

"Oh, wow!" I gasped. I knew the name of course, it was part of the Sandstone legend. John and Judith had been among the original group, which also included Dave Schwind and Oralia Leal, who met at the Williamson's home in the San Fernando Valley before the Williamsons purchased the Ranch. I knew there had been a falling-out between the Williamsons and the Bulleros, but here they were standing in front of me.[i]

That was years before I met her, but she was just as beautiful that night at Sandstone. I got busy greeting other members and guests; it was obviously going to be a good party with over 50 couples attending.

But later, close to midnight, I did find time to leave the door and wander downstairs. I admit I was specifically looking for Judith. And I found her with little trouble. She stood out like a beacon! She and John were sitting on a mattress talking to another couple. The really big difference was that they were nude. Some people lose a bit, some a lot, when they take off their clothes. All their objective physical imperfections become evident. With men, it might be shaggy hair, pot belly, flat ass. With women, it was usually over-weight, loose, flabby skin, sagging breasts, and those lines across the backs of their thighs. Remember, this is my subjective criticism. John and Judith had none of those imperfections. Physically, they were both extremely attractive.

I somewhat boldly sat down on the mattress next to Judith. My position as club manager did have some privileges. Judith glanced over at me and put her hand on my leg. I got goose bumps and she noticed. She smiled, "Tom, wasn't it?"

"Yes."

"How long have you lived here, Tom?"

"About four years." I was staring at her and she noticed.

"I assume you like it?"

"Very much."

"Why?"

I laughed, "You want the recorded answer I give all new members?"

"I want your answer."

I thought a minute. "OK, I like the lifestyle, the value system, the philosophy. What we're trying to accomplish here."

"Not the sex?" she teased.

"What sex?"

She was genuinely surprised. "You don't have sex here?"

"Oh, that!" I laughed again. "Of course I do. But I'm much more interested in quality, not quantity."

She turned to face me and put both hands on my legs. "Does that mean you don't find very much quality sex here?" She was definitely flirting with me now.

"Not much, Judith. Lots of hot sex, which is OK some times, but not much cool sex. I used to think only men were lousy lovers, but since I came here I discovered that a lot of women aren't very good either."

"Ah, a true Romantic. How wonderful! I haven't met one in a long time, and would never expect to find one at Sandstone." She leaned forward and kissed me on the cheek. She smelled so clean!!

"Thank you, Judith," I whispered. There was no doubt about our mutual feelings.

"What time do you – you know – get off work?"

"I'm already off. Any stragglers come in Marty or Sue can handle them. Why?"

Without answering my question, she turned to John. His hands and lips were busy exploring the woman on the other side of him. "John, my love," Judith said, interrupting his fun - and obvious excitement.

"Hummm? What? Oh, Judith."

She kissed him on the shoulder. "I'm staying here tonight."

He smiled, "That's funny. So am I. See you at breakfast." He returned his attentions to the other woman.

"Can we go to your place, Tom?"

"Sure. Let's go." I knew the woman John was interested in. I also knew he wasn't in for nearly as much fun as I was.

Gay Talese described Judith: "Judith's wholesome good looks, and her fair complexion, cheekbones, and short blond hair reminds me of the actress Kim Novak"

❧

Patty

"Hello, Tom?"

"Yes."

"This is Kathy. I was wondering if it would be okay with you if I came down and spend a couple of days there?"

I had to think about that one for a minute. I knew Kathy was up in San Francisco working on a film with her father, and I hadn't seen her for a while. "Sure, Kathy, come on down."

"Great. Could you pick me up at the airport?"

She called me on a Monday, and she was due in Wednesday. Obviously, I didn't know it when I talked to Kathy, but that Wednesday was going to be a very important day in my life – it was the day I met Patty.

Danny and Patty had attended one of Marty's talks, and even though they didn't understand everything he said, they were curious enough to accept his invitation to visit the Retreat.

They seemed to be a nice, friendly couple. They smiled a lot, talked softly, and asked good questions. They were both in good physical shape, especially Patty. She was short, maybe 5'-5", with long reddish-blonde hair, a very slim beautifully proportioned figure, and a lovely smile. Danny was about the same height, slight build, thinning dark hair. They were the type of young couple I was always looking for to join the club. I didn't put on a hard-sell, just let them spend the afternoon doing whatever they liked. The first time I saw Patty nude she was returning from the swimming pool and it was obvious that clothes didn't do her justice.

I asked her, "How'd you like the pool?"

"Oh, it was great! I could spend hours in there."

"Well, why don't you? I have to go down to the city for a while, but you're welcome to stay as long as you like." I really didn't want them to leave, but I had to pick up Kathy at the airport.

On the way to the airport, I thought about Patty, and the woman I was going to pick up, Kathy. She'd told me on the phone she wasn't trying to get something started with me again, she just wanted to relax at the Ranch with John and Barbara and me. If I didn't want her to sleep in my cottage, she'd sleep someplace else. Part of that sounded a little like a Guilt trip, but maybe she was being honest for a change. The woman I'd just left seemed very interesting, and I was looking forward to seeing her when I got back.

Kathy told me about all the hassles they were having up north trying to make the movie while I drove back to the Ranch. Then she asked me how things were at the Ranch. This was the first week in December, and things weren't going well. The members were getting more nervous every weekend, and the family wasn't much better. We knew the sale of the Ranch was going through, we just didn't know when. It was almost impossible to sell memberships under those conditions, so our budget got shot to hell. We tried to reassure people that if the place did sell, they would get a refund on the unused portion of their membership, but it didn't help. They lived in a rip-off society so they knew they'd get ripped off again.

I'd spent a lot of time downstairs the last couple of weeks talking to key members, the ones with the biggest mouths, trying to calm them down, give them accurate information, but it was a waste of time. They continued to turn people off on joining the Retreat, and without memberships we were in trouble. Eventually, it's the reason we closed the club when we did. We just couldn't afford to keep it open, so in their haste, the members were only defeating themselves.

When Kathy and I returned to the Ranch I noticed that one of our new single male members had come up, and was looking for someone to take to the Wednesday pot-luck. He'd complained to me about not being able to find a female to bring to a party, and I'd told him it was best to find a woman down the hill before coming all the way up to the Ranch.

I saw Patty a couple of times that afternoon when she walked through the living room, but I was too busy to talk to her. Then just before supper, she and Danny and the single guy walked in the front door. Danny told me that he and Patty were going to be the single member's guest that evening. There were a few reasons why I couldn't let that happen, mainly because the single guy still didn't have a date. I explained all of that, and Danny and Patty were very apologetic about the confusion. I told them it wasn't their fault, they weren't members yet

156

and didn't know all the rules. So all three of them had to leave. I suggested that Danny and Patty could stay as my guests, but they refused because of the single guy.

I felt bad about them leaving, so when I thought enough time had passed for them to get home, I called them, and asked Danny to come back up as my guests. I explained how the single guy was using them to get in to a party, and Danny finally agreed to return.

After dinner, I found Kathy lying on the floor in front of the fireplace with John. They seemed to be starting a very nice incident, so I took the opportunity to go downstairs and see how the party was going. Since this was Wednesday night, there were newcomers who needed to be watched.

Danny and Patty were lying on the mattress directly across from the stairwell, so I glanced over at them as I went by. They didn't seem to be doing anything, just lying there as if waiting for something to happen. I continued on down to the bar, checking out the action on the mattresses as I passed, and everything appeared to be fine – the start of a good party. There were some very lovely couples and everyone seemed to be involved in positive activities.

I sat down next to a pretty young lady and talked for a few minutes, but I wasn't interested in getting involved with her at the moment. I asked her, "Maybe later? I've got some work to do." She gave me a big smile and a kiss and told me to look for her.

As I walked back toward the stairs, I noticed Patty watching me, so I went over and sat down on the floor beside the mattress. I wanted to make sure I was nonthreatening to Danny, so I didn't sit directly on the mattress. I assume I said something banal to validate my visit, but I don't know what it was. I just remember leaning over and resting my elbows on the mattress and cupping my head in my hands, and Patty leaning toward me in the same position. That's when I realized Patty and I loved each other.

That realization came when I looked in her eyes, read all her signals, and checked my own feelings. There was no doubting the communication that passed between us.

Then I realized something else; someone had brought Alice B. Toklas brownies to the pot-luck!

I'm no stranger to marijuana-laced brownies, they were popular at hippie parties and love-ins in the 60s, but to realize that I was getting stoned that night was almost too much to handle along with the emotional connection to Patty –

which I would have to explore more fully when I came down. Reluctantly, I had to excuse myself and get upstairs quick. We've constantly told our members to not bring drugs onto the premises unless they were already in their bloodstream. That was more a legal judgment than a moral one. Those brownies could get the Retreat closed down if the wrong person ate some and freaked out, and there was a platter full of them sitting on the dining room table for all to sample.

I stashed the platter of brownies, and made the rest of the family members who were in the main house aware of what had happened. I found Kathy still on the living room floor with John, and decided not to bother them. I went back downstairs and started watching the people in the room for signs of unusual behavior as I lay down on the floor beside the mattress where Danny and Patty were still lying. I glanced at her over the edge of the mattress and she seemed to be glad I was back. I was just about to put my head in Patty's lap when Kathy arrived. Unlike me, she wasn't considerate enough to assess the situation and find something else to do. She came over and straddled my butt, then began giving me a back-rub. At another time I would have welcomed it, but between the brownies and Patty, this was sensory overload. I excused myself to the lovely couple on the mattress and took Kathy back upstairs.

We stayed in the living room most of the evening, talking to John and Barbara, then we went over to the cottage about midnight. Kathy wanted to make love, but I didn't. I was still trying to understand what happened earlier between me and Patty. Finally, I got up and was headed toward the door when Kathy said, "You're going back over to fuck that woman, aren't you?"

"I don't think so, Kathy, I'm not even sure they're still there, but I have to go see how everyone else is doing." I didn't tell her about the brownies as I left and I wasn't aware of Kathy following me to the main house.

When I walked into the house, it seemed extraordinarily quiet. No one was in the living room or dining room, so I went downstairs. I saw some people asleep, but none of them were Danny and Patty. I decided they must have left, and went back upstairs to have a cigarette and think.

Out of the corner of my eye, I noticed some movement in the dining room, and thought it was just the ghosts I'd seen before. But when I turned my head to look I saw it was Danny and Patty. They hadn't left. I don't know where they'd been, but it didn't matter.

They came over and joined me, and we started talking. I doubt if any of us remembers what was said, I know I can't. My only reason was to maintain contact with Patty. I haven't talked so much, so fast, since that first time in the pool with Natalie. But this was for a much more positive reason; I wanted to be close to this woman, and talking was all I could do. Danny was beginning to realize what was happening, but he was helpless. It was obvious we weren't going to rip our clothes off and have mad sex right there, but even the non-verbal communication was threatening to him. I admit, I didn't really care about Danny, I was getting a very clear message from Patty – she wanted to be with me.

We talked all night – literally! I made a big pot of coffee which kept me going, and we were still talking when Kathy came into the house looking very dejected, but when she saw the three of us, she brightened. It didn't look like we had a three-way or even a two-way orgy after all.

Danny and Patty left shortly after Kathy arrived, and I didn't see them again for almost a week. I talked to them on the phone a couple of times, and they invited me to supper the following Tuesday.

The dinner was nice, I guess, but once again my memory fails me. I know they lived in an apartment in Brentwood that was a clone of forty thousand other apartments in Los Angeles, and that there was an unused swimming pool outside their front window – which was draped so no one could see in. I remember muttering something about a nightingale singing on a record of Respighi's *Pines of Rome* that was playing, but most of the night is a blank. Patty must have looked beautiful because I stared at her all night.

I probably talked about Sandstone because I really wanted to sell them (her) on the philosophy, value system and lifestyle. I didn't know what kind of relationship we were going to have, but I knew we would have one. I also knew I was a threat to Danny, but he'd just have to handle it. I'm sure he understood what was happening.

The next night, Wednesday, we made love for the first time back at the Ranch. Danny and Patty and Kathy and I were sitting on the floor talking. Actually, Patty and I were talking, and we weren't really aware of what anybody else was doing. We still had our clothes on, for some silly reason, and we knew all the talking was meaningless. We had to touch each other and much more intimately than just holding hands. Finally, I just took her hand and walked downstairs. Like Jane said, "If you have to ask, forget it."

We undressed in the ballroom vestibule, then went over to the empty mattress and made love. I'm sure we were both trying to put so much of ourselves into the act (Reason 2: If you really want to know someone.), the sex

159

act was simply the best way we could get close to each other. It didn't seem to last very long, and didn't live up to our expectations – if we could explain what those were.

When we returned upstairs Patty went directly over to Danny, and I sat next to Kathy. I don't know about Danny (I found out much later he totally freaked! That was confusing, because he told me he worked as a sexual surrogate, see R. J. Noonan: Sex Surrogates: A Clarification of Their Functions, so his freak out was a bit hypocritical; he could have sex with other women under the guise of therapy, but Patty couldn't have sex under the honesty of her emotions), but Kathy was having trouble handling it. She was very hurt and wanted to know what Patty had that she didn't. That wasn't even a fair question.

"Well, I can't stand this," she announced, "I'm going home." She went in the dining room and spoke to Danny and Patty for a minute and she left.

The rest of the night was a blank. I don't know what Danny and Patty did. I do remember making arrangements to accompany them to a Family Synergy meeting Friday night (see Family Synergy - Polyamory in Southern California). Doug drove me down to their apartment because my car broke down (we accept the reality that cars not working is part of the value system), and Danny had agreed to drive me back up to the Ranch.

The Family Synergy meeting was as boring as previous meetings had been that I attended, and if it weren't for Patty, I would have left after the first ten minutes or never gone in the first place. It's one of those organizations that is supposedly interested in alternative lifestyles, but they only give lip-service to it, and forming committees to explore various possibilities to report back. They're bogged down in bureaucracy as solidly as Washington D.C. (Months later I was invited to lecture before the group. They almost lynched me when I told them casual family nudity, including children, in the home was a good thing, and don't close bedroom doors during sex!)

Anyway, I held on to Patty during the business (?) part of the meeting; then we broke up into smaller groups to play games (Games?). I was with Patty in the first group, then we were supposed to change partners for the next game so I picked a group where I could at least watch her. She had such a quiet, serene look. We finally finished the banal game-playing and left for the much-publicized party held after every meeting. Maybe that's where the talk stops and the action begins.

No such luck! Just more talk on a one-on-one basis, so I talked to Patty. This time, I gave her the hard-sell on Sandstone. When I stopped to breathe, she told me, "Tom, I don't understand half of what you're saying, but it sounds beautiful." Wonderful! I was beginning to get through to her.

Then Danny started feeling "Time Jealousy," so she went back to him. There was nobody else I wanted to talk to, and they all had their clothes on anyway, so I left.

Leaving that party was one of the dumbest things I ever did. I headed for the biggest street around and stuck out my thumb. After fifteen minutes, I got a ride with a Gay looking for a blow job. When I let him know how straight I was, he remembered someplace else he had to be and dropped me off. I knew this was sheer idiocy, so I walked across the street and stuck my thumb out again. I was going back to the party and hoping that Danny and Patty were still there.

They were gone. By then, I felt I couldn't do anything right, but I took a big chance and called them at home. "Hello, Danny."

"Where are you?"

"At what's left of the party."

"Stay there, I'll be right over."

I found out later than she went into shock for a little while when I left, and then started crying. That's why they left the party.

It took Danny longer than I expected to come get me, because he ran out of gas. When he did arrive, his first question was, "Why did you leave?"

"All I can say is it seemed like a good idea at the time."

"Well, we've got to get this mess straightened out. Patty's a wreck. Will you come back to the apartment and talk about it?"

"Sure, why not." I think I was falling into the martyr role.

When we arrived at the apartment, Patty was sitting on the couch nude. This wasn't going to be easy.

Danny asked, "Okay, what are we going to do?"

"If you want to, you can drive me back to the Ranch and I won't bother you two again."

"That's not what I want," Patty told us.

"Then I'll put it another way," I told them. "I want to have a relationship with Patty. It can be a Primary or a Satellite. Take your pick."

"How about it, Danny?"

"Wait a minute," Patty said. "don't I have something to say about this?"

"Danny?"

"Hey, wait a minute! I've had a Primary relationship with Danny, I haven't had one with you, Tom. How do I know which of you I want to live with if I don't have a valid framework to judge by. That's like saying I can have one of two cupcakes, but I only get to taste one before I buy." I liked her metaphor. I found out later she had been a member of MENSA.

"I've got to think about this," Danny told us. "I don't think any of us are in shape to make decision tonight. Come on, Tom, I'll drive you home."

I slept very well that night, knowing I'd given it my best shot. Patty finally called the next afternoon. "I want to come up and see you, Tom."

"I'll be waiting."

It took her over an hour to get to the Ranch, and when she walked in, it was obvious she hadn't slept much. She still looked damn good.

"I want to have a Primary relationship with you, Tom."

Potpourri

In my five years at Sandstone I met a lot of people in a very unique social environment. Some of those people had very little impact on me, and others made a lifelong impression. I didn't make a lot of personal contacts until I was living at the Ranch, and then managing the Retreat. Obviously, my association with the other family members was on a more continual basis than with members of the club. I do have the distinction of never having sexual relations with another family member – except ones actually living with me. I was more intimate with club members, some of whom I loved very much. Here are a few examples of the ones I remember:

H.G. was a gentleman in the truest sense of the word. He had the class and poise of Adolphe Menjou, a classic actor from the past. He was from an earlier era with his fancy dress and Rolls-Royce. He was also killing himself slowly with booze until we started giving him some honest feedback. When I threatened him with expulsion if he didn't lighten up, he responded by sobering up. It was beautiful to watch.

162

Lovely June. Another person with a lot of class in a society where such character is no longer appreciated. She and H.G. remind me of Don Quixote and Aldonza Dulcinea – beautiful people in a time warp.

June embarrassed me one night when I walked over to her to say hello, and she suddenly put her hand on my chest. It was as if she'd suddenly discovered the sense of touch. "Oh, my God! That feels so good," she announced as she caressed my chest and stomach. It caught me completely off guard.

"Hey, Carol, come and feel this man's skin. It's marvelous!" So Carol had to come over and caress my chest. I never thought of my skin as being so special and still don't. But it certainly impressed those two ladies. After a few others joined in the fun, I managed to excuse myself and return upstairs.

In the variety of our membership, there were a few people who never experienced the nighttime activities, but the majority of them never saw the Retreat in the daytime. Steve was one of the daytime members. He came up regularly on most Tuesdays, spend a few hours, and leave. While he was there he might go for a swim, lie on the grass or sit in the living room and talk to us. He was a very pleasant man who always brought something with him; it might have been breakfast pastries, pizza or a bottle of wine. It was always a pleasure to see him because we knew there was no need to keep an eye on him. Never once did he get pushy with anyone.

Bud and Joan joined the club shortly after I became manager, and we enjoyed watching and taking part in each other's experiences for the full year they were members. Most members only used about four months of their annual membership, but Bud and Joan stuck it out for the entire year, and would have renewed if we'd stayed open. They would definitely be considered two of the "beautiful people" at Sandstone.

When Bud first arrived at the Ranch for an interview, I suspected that he might be employed in some form of law enforcement – we did have a few such members, some undercover, some not. It turned out I wasn't even close. At first, he seemed to be on a total, chauvinistic candy store trip and made no bones about it. He didn't bother telling Joan too much about Sandstone before he brought her up for their first party, and she was surprised by what she walked into. I asked her what her first impression had been.

163

"Oh, it didn't really bother me too much," she replied, "I walked in and the first thing I saw was this guy [me] walking toward me with his cock dangling between his legs and a big smile on his face. Didn't bother me. Not much!" We both laughed.

Bud and Joan went through some very heavy changes in their year at the Retreat. Bud finally understood the difference between "hot" and "cool" sex, and also experienced Fear of Loss. Joan found out what it meant to be more liberated as a person and a woman than she'd ever imagined. Bud had been the first and only man she had sex with, even though he was prone to 'play around' and made no bones about admitting it. For her to be capable of the same thing was a little difficult for her to grasp. It took time, and some pain, on both their parts before she really blossomed.

They invited me down to their home in the Pacific Palisades, and even invited a lovely young lady to dine with me. Since I was in their environment, I waited to see if they were going to initiate any Sandstone type activity – like casual nudity. They didn't, but it was still a pleasant evening.

There was Jerry who got the nickname, "Midnight Skulker," and we did have to keep an eye on him. One night he was on a mattress with a woman, and a man came over and started getting in on his action. "Hey, man," he told him without missing a stroke, "Go find your own old lady."

The newcomer responded, "This is my 'old lady – I'm her husband."

Jerry let out a soft moan and rolled off the mattress.

He got his nickname from trying to sneak up on unsuspecting females who were asleep. We considered that "obnoxious behavior" and had to cancel his membership.

There was enormous Jean Pierre, the Great White Hunter from Africa who could – and did – satisfy three women at the same time, and with only one hand! He lost the other one in a dynamite accident when he was trying to feed the pygmy tribe by throwing a stick of dynamite in the lake to stun fish.

And then there was beautiful, lovable, always excited Jeremy – one of the few men at Sandstone I truly loved, as did anyone else who met him.

Jeremy's first encounter with Sandstone happened in the first year of the Retreat's operation, and was an extremely profound experience for him. At the time, he wasn't doing well as an actor or a husband. He was holed up in a small

164

attic room in Venice, California, spending most of the time with a bottle in his hand. A writer for one of the Southern California sensationalistic Magazines had been assigned to do a story on Sandstone, and didn't want to go alone. So she called Jeremy, who she knew from his TV career and recent divorce, and told him to get dressed they were going to a party, and she'd pick him up.

During the hour long trip up to the Ranch, she told Jeremy as much as she could about the place they were headed for, which wasn't much, and the more she talked the more nervous Jeremy got. He heard words like "orgies" and "fuck club" and "sexual equality," and he started making excuses to stop. He needed a bathroom, or had to make a phone call to his agent, anything that might delay their arrival. I might add here that his behavior was a complete role reversal; usually it was the women who go through that kind of fear when they hear where they're going.

Then Jeremy started asking himself some questions; "What can happen to me? Are these people going to do me serious bodily harm or kill me? Whips? Chains? Doesn't sound like it. So what the hell am I afraid of?"

That was Friday evening. When they finally left Sunday night, Jeremy was ecstatic! Neither of them had slept during that time, and had very little to eat. There was just too much going on, too many wonderful people, to worry about details like food and sleep. Jeremy got answers to some of his questions, but not all.

I happened to be in the Westwood office the next day when Jeremy came bounding in with a ten-mile wide smile. He still hadn't slept, but it certainly didn't show. He had to have a membership in that place! As he filled out the application, he said, "I'm not sure what the hell is going on up there, but I definitely have to find out!"

He did find out and I'm sure he would admit that it changed his whole life. His professional career took an about-face when he landed a good role in a daily soap opera, and his personal life improved considerably when he met an equally beautiful person, Sally, at the Retreat. They enjoyed a long relationship.

Jeremy was very interested in motion pictures as a means of communication (he'd made a few, like *Sons of Katie Elder, The Born Losers* and *Hell's Angels '69*), and one of his big concerns at that time, maybe it still is, was to photograph two people making love. The problem, as he saw it, was to film it in such a way as to not give the impression they were just having sex. As far as I know, neither he nor anyone else has done a very good job of it. Jeremy told me that he felt it

165

wouldn't be possible until the advent of home videos. That way people can enhance their viewing pleasure by creating their own environment. He even told me he might publish a booklet to go along with the video.

Two of my all-time favorite people in my years at Sandstone were Dale and Carol, who only visited us for a few days the last two months we were open. It was practically love at first sight! I can't remember two people who enjoyed Sandstone more. At the parties they were both in the Candy Store, but probably Carol more than Dale. She just couldn't get enough. They had a zest for living that I rarely saw at the Retreat.

And wild, wonderful Betty Dodson from New York. She never understood what a non-swinger, me, was doing managing a swing club. I gave up trying to explain the difference between a swing club and Sandstone to her. She found two short-comings at the Retreat; not enough men, and not enough experimentation. "Everybody just does it the same old way!" Of course, she was only there for a very short time, and missed a few of the freakier parties.

There was a couple we rarely saw upstairs, except in the kitchen occasionally. They'd come to a party, go in the side door downstairs, undress and proceed to the Ballroom. She'd come out, find a partner and take him back in to the Ballroom where her husband was lying. She would have sex with the man while her husband watched. That's not too unusual, except that we watched them one night, and discovered that she was with a different guy every six minutes. We also saw her husband reach over and punch her in the mouth – not too gently. We decided that was to let her know the six minutes were up.

"Somebody stole my bananas! How am I supposed to get my potassium?" This outburst came from the kitchen one Sunday morning when one of our members discovered his cherished bananas were gone. George was usually a quiet man who usually arrived on Friday night with his wife or girlfriend (we stopped trying to determine which one was actually his wife), and his little black bag, and set up camp in a corner of the Ballroom for the weekend. His 'camp' included a portable spotlight with a rotating color wheel, and spraying the whole room with Hi Karate after-shave. The only problem we ever had with George was that he talked constantly from the minute he arrived until he left – yes, even while having sex.

166

Earth Mother Eleanor – what a very special woman! She taught Yoga classes in the beginning. She lived at the Ranch for a few weeks while her house was being refurbished, and she would be up ay six in the morning, when some of us were heading for a bed after the party, doing her yoga on the front lawn. Then she would jog around the perimeter for about an hour before starting the housework. She still holds the record for being the oldest woman I made love with – and definitely one of the best!

So many people! It would take volumes to describe all the ones who left an impression on me. Each day was unique, we never knew what to expect. It was certainly different than going to work at the same building, in the same cubicle, with the same people forty hours a week. I didn't like to leave the Ranch for more than a few hours, because I knew I'd miss something. One phone call could start a chain reaction that could affect all of us for days.

One of the best parts of the Monday Night Meeting was the "munchy" part, some dessert one of us made. Sue decided she'd make chocolate chip cookies. She worked all afternoon on them, and when she took the cookie sheet out of the oven, there was one giant cookie spread all over the cookie sheet. That didn't stop us from breaking off pieces and eating them. Doug asked her what she'd put in them.

"Just the regular stuff the recipe called for."

"What kind of flour did you use, Sue?"

"I don't know. That big bag in the back cupboard. Why?"

"Ha! That explains it. That's not flour."

We all stopped eating a second and asked in unison, "What is it?"

"Pancake mix!" We went back to eating.

Jonathan came out of the kitchen one night with a big bowl of something, and sat down next to John. John looked over at the bowl with hungry anticipation. "What's that, Jon?"

"Mashed potatoes with cranberry sauce on top," Jonathan replied.

John looked like he was going to throw up on the coffee table for a minute, and lost his appetite.

The night I was downstairs with Joan, while Bud was busy elsewhere, trying to loosen her up a little and making progress. Another woman, Jeanette, came over and tapped me on the shoulder. "Tom, I hate to tell you this, but there's a guy laying on the bottom of the swimming pool. I think he's dead."

I jumped up and headed for the side door, then I saw Marty and Sue on a mattress right next to the door. Well, somebody did it to me, so...

"Marty, I hate to tell you this, but...

Fortunately, the guy didn't die, but when I called 911, we ended up with a parade of official vehicles; three sheriff's cars, a Highway Patrol car, two rescue trucks and one ambulance. We always got good service on party nights.

When I took one of the officers down to the house to get the man's records, we went in the bedroom and there was Sue – naked, of course. The officer was obviously uncomfortable, but when she couldn't find the man's records right away, she began rubbing her breasts – a nervous habit of hers. That was more than the officer could handle.

John went to the L.A. County Sheriff's office in Malibu before they opened the Retreat, and told them exactly what they were going to do, and that if any of their deputies ever wanted a cup of coffee, to drop by – the pot was always on. It was fun to watch the expressions on some deputy's faces on a Saturday night with a parade of naked bodies walking through the kitchen.

Sandstone was a giant hall of mirrors. Those of us living there received feedback from each other and from the members on their sporadic visits to the Retreat. They brought their value systems and lifestyles with them, reminding us of where we had been and why we were here now.

They were a cross-section of the society we wanted to change, but the only way that could happen was for the individuals to change – we couldn't change them. That was one of the main functions of Sandstone, to be a role model for a successful alternative lifestyle, and give them the opportunity to experience that lifestyle in a safe, supportive environment. It would have been great if we could have a hundred people living at the Ranch, but we didn't have the facilities. If our family exceeded ten people, we started feeling the pinch. Even so, there was a lot of the Sandstone philosophy that people could take back down the hill and incorporate into their own lifestyle.

When I visited members in their homes, I didn't see as much of that as I would have liked, but that meant they would have to live up to my expectations, which I had no right to do. Of course, they had their expectations of Sandstone, and we didn't always live up to those. Some people didn't like the way I ran the club, but I did what I felt was in the best interests of Sandstone and the individuals.

The last party we had was big! There were close to 150 people attending, some of them members we hadn't seen for months.

It kept me very busy at the door. At times there were four or five couples waiting to get registered. At one point I was trying to get some guest cards filled out when I noticed a very lovely young lady standing behind the others who kept smiling at me. I smiled back, but didn't recognize her until she called, "Tom! It's me!" Then I really looked at her. It was my oldest step-daughter. She turned 18 a month earlier, and took advantage of it by attending our final party. I gave her a warm hug and a kiss, unaware of the other couple who were with her. They seemed very nice, and I proudly introduced them as my daughter and her friends. We were standing by the bar and I asked her, "What do you think?"

"Just about what I imagined, Tom."

We stayed downstairs talking for a bit, then the five of us returned to the living room. I was a little disappointed that Menissa and her friends declined to take their clothes off or participate in any activity, but I'd always emphasized Optionality to her and the others. They left to visit Janice in the West House.

The party was still going strong when I left about two-thirty. I just couldn't get into the party mood.

These have been random thoughts and memories about the people I met at Sandstone, but I doubt if I've been able to convey the full meaning of the effect they had on me. It involves emotions that don't translate into words except by using esoteric metaphors which I don't do. The experience of sitting in the living room listening to people like Bob Francoeur and David Halberstam talking is exciting, but it just doesn't read very well. Words are too inadequate to describe events at a good Saturday night party, or a walk around the property at night. When people, especially writers, asked us to explain Sandstone we could only tell them that Sandstone was ninety percent experiential. The lessons of Sandstone could be learned, but they couldn't be taught.

Diary, Fall of 1972

Tues. Aug. 8, 1972

Had a long talk with Jon and Bunny Dana last night, and brought them up to date on most things. Couple of points came out: Much more difficult for females to adapt to this lifestyle than males. Much bigger acceptance problem due to insecurity and expectations. Also, it's a very difficult environment to work on a relationship. Most, if not all, couples who have lived here haven't taken the time to build a strong primary before starting to experiment. And as soon as they do that, it weakens the primary. Once again, it's due to expectations and opportunity. The expectations aren't real.

Nanci arrived about 3:30. No vibes from her, so I told her Jon and Bunny were back. She went to their room to talk. Later, we talked, and she told me Dale, her dad, had asked her to move in with them, and he wants to put her through college. She was very excited about that.

Thurs. Aug. 17, 1972

Obviously, I haven't written anything for a while. I've had no contact with Nanci since the 8th. Pamela came up last Wednesday, the 9th, and we had a 'nice' time. We made love in the afternoon, but it was too short. She stayed overnight, but she left the Pot Luck shortly after supper. Later that same night, I got together with Ann. That's developed into something of a problem. Percy is having trouble handling the situation – experiencing fear of loss. We haven't done anything since that night, but she comes up almost every afternoon. I think she understands how I feel about her. Tuesday, a cuckoo named Lynn came up expecting to move in for a couple of months – thanks to Floyd. I got her out of the house and over to the cottage, then I calmed her down and told her she couldn't move in. One of the worst I ever had.

Wednesday was quite a day. I was getting frustrated about getting Nanci's picture blown up, and then walking back to the house from the darkroom I found a $10.00 bill in the driveway. A very nice girl named Lynn, not the cuckoo, came up. We spent a nice afternoon together, then she drove me down to the camera store. I put the 35mm slide in for a print and paid for it. Then we went to the music store and bought some tapes. Before the Pot Luck started, we got into a pretty heavy scene, but couldn't do anything about it due to time. Then when I *did have time, she had to leave. She told me, "I want to come back when there aren't people here so you and I can spend some time together." So we agreed she'd come back next Tuesday afternoon. I have to be careful – she'd be easy to love. Also mailed a letter to Nanci. She should get it Friday. Later, at the party, went sixty-nine with Leslie – very good! Pamela came up today and we made love. It was pretty good. I'm still not completely in shape, but it's lasting longer and feeling better. Maybe this week-end will do it. Had a good talk with John and Barbara about the Idaho project. Marty and Sue stayed in the bedroom until they left, then Sue asked me some questions. I told her if she wanted to know anything about their plans, talk to them. Her response was, "Yeah, sure!" Very bad vibes between the four of them. Looks like someone may be leaving, maybe both. John told me he's planning a core group of about six for the project.*

Wed. Aug. 23, 1972

Let's go back to Friday. I got very uptight with Bill R. and Alex Comfort showing up alone. Had a talk with Bill Saturday morning, and explained how a person's perception of Sandstone changes depending on the commitment they bring here. Since he wasn't bringing any, his writing was strictly from the singles viewpoint. He understood. Don't know what to do about Alex. I talked to Barbara about it Friday afternoon, which I apologized for later. I told her there were enough people here I can talk to. Friday night I got a thing going with Judith, Floyd's date. Not so good. It seems like the more sex I have the fewer females I find who know how to do it right. Almost everyone since Nanci, and Camille before her. Leslie came back up Saturday and started a heavy transfer trip on me, then Pamela showed up looking great. She stayed until Sunday afternoon. I had a long talk with her and Jim Borden Saturday night. Monday night was pretty boring. I ate too much, and also became aware of how Janice refuses to turn me on. I was looking forward to seeing Lynn Tuesday. She came up in the afternoon, and after some head-tripping, we had fun. She kind of freaked me out when she screamed. Kathy came up later. I can't remember how it started, but the three of us got into a very heavy trip. Lynn really liked Kathy and Kathy liked me. Kathy wasn't completely comfortable with Lynn's attentions, so she stayed very close to me. This upset Lynn enough that she was going to home. The three of us went to the cottage and talked. Then we went for a swim and then back to the house. Jonathan came in and joined us. He and Bunny had a fight (another one), and Bunny had left. Jonathan called this morning from Hollywood. I took

171

some photos of Lynn, she was back in a good mood. Kathy is coming back up tonight, and so is Leslie. Ann is here now. It's getting complicated. Marty and Sue went to the beach again. Looks like it's going to be a good party tonight. Marty pulled a power trip on Jeanette last night. He wanted to get into it with us, but Sue came out and cooled that.

Fri. Aug. 25, 1972

Kathy has been sleeping here since Tuesday; very heavy fusion. She refuses to read my signals and listen to my words (except what she wants to hear). So I finally made it very clear this morning; she was forcing me to reject her. She got me so upset I actually called her Nanci. She kept trying to compare the relationships, but I'm not. Wednesday night Ann told me she wasn't "in love" with me anymore. I told her good, now maybe we could be friends. She replied that it would be interesting to see if she could "like" me now. Pamela came up Thursday afternoon. Nothing special happened. Got Nanci's picture back, can't decide whether I like it or not. Still have a rapport with Barbara, but I'm still lonely. I don't know if I can find someone to have a relationship with, but I can see I'll have to be more careful about who I choose to have fun with. Wednesday night I signed in about 56 people, and after looking them over, I told Barbara, "Congratulations. You're the only woman here tonight. All the rest are still little girls." She naturally agreed. She told me this morning that she and John are going to find a girl for them. She relates better to females than males.

Sat. Aug. 26, 1972

I haven't heard from Kathy, but Carol talked to her after she left here, and told me Kathy was very upset. She just has too much baggage for me; it would require more energy than I can give it right now. She asked me what type of woman was I looking to fall in love with, and my only answer was that I wasn't in love with her. I had fun with a girl named Karen that Floyd brought up last night, and it flashed on me how I'm counting – and I don't like it. I'm going to have to be more selective. Still haven't heard from Nanci. Still looking forward to hearing from her. Got very stoned last night with Jon and Bunny. They made some interesting comments about John and Barbara, and Marty and Sue. Now, it's late, I've seen everybody who is coming up and I'm bored. So I'm sitting here listening to Procol Harum, wishing someone would come over.

172

Mon. Aug. 28, 1972

No meeting, no nothing. Marty and Sue stayed in their bedroom. Kathy came up yesterday evening. She had a long talk with John and Barbara, and tried to put me down. I had to stop that before it got vicious. We had fun last night listening to music, and she told me she's keeping a very good journal. I'm really not in love with her, and that doesn't upset me. I know what I want now, and she just doesn't measure up. It's the intangibles that are missing. I saw Pamela this afternoon, and it really felt good just to hold her close. We did make love later. I called Julie this afternoon, and set up a date for next week. I'm tired of starting new relationships. I want to work on one, not just start it. I'm tired, bored, and lonely. I'm even bored writing.

What's the scariest thing ever happened to you? I've had a few in my long life, but I think this one tops them all: 3:00 AM, it was a good party, got some strong smoke, laying on the bed nude listening to Pink Floyd. Suddenly aware a 6-inch, black-and-yellow tarantula is on the bed. Shit! I didn't feel any fear, I was mesmerized watching it. Beautiful creature! One little bite and I'd be dead. What to do! Before I can decide, I feel its claws as it climbs up on my thigh, then down, then up on my other thigh, then down on the bed. Goes over to other side of the bed and leaves. What the fuck just happened!

Fri. Sept. 1, 1972

Marty made sure I understood that he and Sue would appreciate it if I wouldn't let, or take, people into their bedroom. He was referring to last night. I started to tell him I had nothing to do with it, but changed my mind. He had me in his sights and wasn't going to be swayed by anything I said. If I'd told him it was Jonathan's idea, he'd have come up with something else. John was there, and he knows the whole story. Marty's very uptight this afternoon because Jim is here, and he and Sue are getting along well. Big weekend starting, maybe something will happen.

Mon. Sept. 4, 1972

The weekend is over and things keep changing. I invited a couple up Saturday night in hopes they'd join. Also, I wanted to see the girl, Ann, again. They'd first come up Tuesday afternoon. Unfortunately, I got busy Saturday night, and they got involved with Bernie and Judith. By the time I got loose, they were busy. I watched her all night, and she was doing what she thought she should do instead of what she wanted to do. I had a little time to talk to her later, but she wouldn't look at me. When I asked her about it, she said my look was too intense – like I was looking inside her. I told her I was, and I was also trying to convey how I felt about her. She said it scared her; another scared person. I'm going to call her tomorrow. Later that night, I talked to a girl Jim brought up named Kristine. She proceeded to tell me that all she was interested in was getting to know me better. We finally got together about 4:30 AM. It must have been intense, because a few people mentioned it to me Sunday. She spent Sunday night and Monday with me. From all the feedback I'm getting, it seems I'm considered a pretty good lover. I just never thought of it before. My goal has always been to please the women I've been with, and I guess I've succeeded. Kris would also like to move in with me. Same old problem – she's a very nice little girl. Really fun to be with, but not enough there for a commitment. John and Barbara are leaving tomorrow for a two-week trip to Idaho. I'm not happy they're leaving again, but I'll handle it. Marty and Sue are close together, but cut off from the rest of us. Jonathan and Bunny are cut off from each other. That's going to leave Janice and me and we're just buddies. Just took a break, and went for one of the freakiest night walks I've ever taken. I saw the two "monks" sitting out on the point; saw and heard the raccoons by the house, and just as I walked by the North house, a coyote howled right beside the West house. Sue laid a heavy rap on Jonathan Saturday night, then Jonathan laid one on Bunny, then Bunny came back to the party and laid one on me. I'm back in the Dr. Tom role. I should stay out of it, but just can't. I probably know more about the different trips people are on here than anybody – including my own. Marty and Sue are the only ones who won't talk too much, but their trip is still visible. They'll probably open up when John and Barbara leave. I'm doing blow-ups for Francoeur's new book, and keep seeing photos of Nanci. I guess the fantasy trip is still alive.

Tues. Sept. 5, 1972

Once again I started watching "The Sandpiper" on TV, and once again I turned it off. This time, I got as far as right after they made love. Very profound and deep feeling of anxiety. I knew where it was going; a deep, beautiful love corrupted and stymied by society. Earlier tonight, I was trying to finish the blow-ups for Francoeur's book, but couldn't get them done. I got very uptight and

174

bummed out trying to do the ones taken downstairs. Barbara was pretty upset when Nancy didn't even call to tell her she wasn't going with them. Barbara told me they asked her what she wanted, and after she told them, they told her what was involved and she agreed. I just went back over these notes and can find no mention of John and Barbara's Nancy. She's been here once, I think it was a week ago. She came up with Marty, then he went back and got Karen. Nancy went directly to John, then they took her up to The Toad. That just about freaked Sue! Barbara said later that Nancy would be going on their trip, but she chickened out. Marty got very physical with Marty S.'s Karen Saturday night on the couch; scared her pretty bad. They haven't been back since. I called Danny and Ann, and they can't afford to join right now.

Saturday, Sept. 9, 1972

I have to go back to Wednesday. Sue and I got into a very heavy conversation about her behavior and mine. She was upset over the girls like Kathy, Ann, Lynn, etc. who go through the heavy transfer on me. I told her it was their fantasy trip, and that I didn't encourage it. The problem was that I didn't treat them like Marty does. She couldn't disagree with that. I spent most of the time in the darkroom until Jim and Kristine arrived. It felt good to see her again. We spent the night together. She's still here today, and neither of us is interested in her leaving. Wednesday night was a very nervous party. Kris and I stayed close together, but talked to other people. A couple of girls came on to me, but I wasn't interested. Part of the reason were the vibes I was getting from Kris. We've talked about it a little, although she hasn't said a word about her feelings regarding me with someone else, although she did say that if she gets turned on by someone, she's going to act on it. I got the feeling she isn't ready for me to be with another girl. That's fine with me right now, she's more than enough, but I do feel that we're going to expand later. I don't think either of us wants it to be a big deal. I'm very happy she's staying here. I'm beginning to think the "little girl" thing is only superficial; kind of a role she's playing to keep from getting hurt. I've seen glimpses of a real woman. So in many ways, she's the type of woman I'm looking for, but she's still holding back. It felt good to realize I'm not afraid to love again, and to admit that love to her. Marty and I are locking horns daily now. He's continually finding some reason to start an argument.

175

Wednesday, Sept. 13, 1972

A kind of down day. I talked to Bob Francoeur last night, and he informed me that he only found one photo out of all the ones I sent him that he likes. A lot of time, energy and some money wasted. I don't think he really knows what he wants – could be his fantasy trip. Heard about Guy Jay purposefully O.D.ing. Hit me a little hard, he was a fantastic artist. Kris has been working to make things better in the cottage. She's going down the hill tonight to talk to her mom and get some personal stuff. That's kind of a commitment, but I'd like to see more. Our relationship is definitely good right now, but it seems like neither of us is looking very far ahead. In some ways, she's holding back more now than last week. I think she realizes it's commitment time.

Thursday, Sept. 14, 1972

What a day! I was walking over to the house, wondering why Kris hadn't called, when I flashed on a baby in the living room. Then the front door opened and a woman came out who I thought was Sue at first. She said, "Good morning!" I replied, "Hi," still wondering about Kris. She came toward me and said, "How are you today?" That didn't sound like Sue. It was Camille! What a surprise. We talked about it and laughed as we entered the house. I was looking up at the pool building when another car drove in, and I told her, "Looks like another surprise." In a few minutes, Nanci walked in. She's really having trouble. Her dad, Dale, has backed down on everything he promised her when she moved in with him. I wonder if he... never mind. She has to move out of the house, get a student loan, and a job. Now for Kris; Jim took her down to her mother's house yesterday afternoon to get some clothes. She told him she might stay overnight, but that she'd call me one way or another. The other was that I'd go down and get her. It's now 8:00, and I haven't heard from her. Finally, about 5:30, I called the Burbank police and asked if they'd check out the address. I waited until 7:00, then called them back. They told me they'd given her mother the message for her to call me. Her mother told them Kris wasn't there, but she knew where she was and she was alright. That sounded even less like Kris. Now I'm really confused. If she's alright, then I'm also irritated. Why didn't she call? I had a long talk with Marcelle last night. We agreed to meet this weekend. Doug seemed pretty uptight when they left. Right now, I'm feeling sadder for Nanci than Kris, because Kris is an unknown. There are two possible reasons she didn't call: either she can't or she doesn't want to. If it's the former, I won't know until

176

I go out to her mother's in the morning. If it's the latter, then it's a free-will decision, and I can't feel sad about that until I know for sure. Nanci called tonight, sounding very unhappy. She's trapped by circumstances. Dale is completely blowing it as a person, and more importantly, as a father. For that, I can really hate him, but at the moment I'm completely helpless with regard to both Nanci and Kris. If Kris isn't calling because she doesn't want to, then she's afraid of the commitment. I've got to go out there in the morning and resolve it.

Sun. Sept. 17, 1972

Sunday afternoon and still no word from Kris. Also no contact with Doug, which does worry me a little. Talked to Jim yesterday evening, but he's too busy going to the beach and napping to go out and check on her. I tried calling this morning, but no answer. Had a very nice time with Marcelle last night, twice. I'm not worried about a transfer. Marty and Sue went to Tijuana today, and they're supposed to leave Tuesday for two weeks at Bill's. They're in much better shape without John and Barbara being here. With such a small group here, it's hard to reject them. John and Barbara can do it, because they don't have to relate to them on a business level. When they're here, they go through me. Tom K. and Dee: Dee is going through some wonderful changes, and Tom K. is still insisting on acceptance, same as Leslie whom I've almost cut off all positive contact with. Tom K. still watches me when he's in the room, and gets visibly uptight when Dee even talks to me. Last night, Dee and I were having a nice talk when she admitted that she didn't like me at first, but she does now. Suddenly, two people forced their way in to our space. Tom K. got protective with Dee, and Leslie sat on the arm of the couch, reaching in between us for the ash tray. Dee had a long talk with Bunny this morning, and Bunny reiterated a lot of the same things I'd told her. We both tried to tell her gently that she had to get away from Tom. She'll realize it eventually. He isn't making any progress, and blocking her from making some. I'm still having trouble relating to Janice because of Michael. I can't get close to him, and don't really want to. It will be interesting to see John and Barbara's reaction to him. Dale came up last night, and I couldn't even be nice to him. He's lucky I didn't bounce him off the walls.

Monday, Sept. 18, 1972.

Late night, can't sleep, coming down off some grass. Still no word from Kris. I went to her mom's house Sunday evening, and she said everything was okay,

177

but wouldn't tell me where she was. Haven't heard from Jim either. They might be together. It looks like she was more "little girl" than I thought. So I'm alone again. How many times do I have to give love before I find someone strong enough to accept it? John and Barbara are right in rejecting those who can't love. They've been though it too many times: Frank and Terri, Marty and Mag, and now Marty and Sue. That's the real history of Sandstone – the people that have tried and failed to live here. Originally, it was the five; John and Barbara, Dave and Oralia and Albert. Actually, there was a Gail Williamson before Albert. There were a few others before, but they didn't live here. Then Frank and Terri, Marty and Mag. It stayed that way for a while, except for a few girls who shared Albert's bedroom like Jenny from Missouri, Natalie, etc. Then it started breaking down. First Dave and Oralia left, that was a big blow to John and Barbara. Next, Frank and Terri, not so bad because Mag was here by then. I lost track there for a while, but some of the names are Kristen and Jaime, Steve and Judith and Michael. Kristen and Jaime were asked to leave. Then there was Sondra, Jaime and Anders. Next Michael and Janice and Sheri, then Butch and Sherry, then me I came before Sondra, Tutt and Marcia and Tanya, Michael's new girlfriend to make the West house a complete mess. Then Jonathan and Bunny, Sue replaced Mag, then Nanci. Doug came before Sue I think. I won't count Diane and Kristine – too short a time. How many people does that make in my time? 31 people since April of 1969. Now, there are ten of us: John and Barbara, Marty and Sue, Jon and Bunny, me, Doug and Janice with little Sheri. It's a very unstable family. How and why they came to Sandstone, what happened to them here, why they left, and what has happened to them since is the real story. On a more superficial level, there's a story behind every one of the thousands who have come to Sandstone for however long they were here.

Tues. Sept. 19, 1972

Marty just had to pick a fight with me this morning soon as he walked out of the bedroom. Yesterday, it was Bunny. Doug is back, which makes all of us happy. The bad news is that when Doug called from the airport, about 1:00 AM, Marty refused to go get him! T he rest of us can't believe it. That's in contradiction to everything we believe on the level of Security Needs. Doug had to hitchhike to Tuna Canyon, then walk up here from the highway in the middle of the night. That means none of us can depend on Marty, and Sue, to help fill those Needs. It could be the proverbial "straw." I've had the strangest feeling all

178

day and evening that Kris was going to walk in the door any minute. Bunny and I got into some interesting speculation about that. Like, what would happen if she showed up with her clothes and stuff? If she just admitted she was scared? What would I do? I think I'd be a fool to turn her away. She's an extraordinary female, but what's her game? I can fantasize about it, and it's something I'll have to handle if it happens. Jim Borden came up and we had a good chat, then Bud and Joan and Frank S. came up. More good talks. The six of us are in a pretty good place right now. It should be the same when John and Barbara get back. It's just Marty and Sue. We've got to resolve that soon. Frank wants to help on Corinne's book of poetry. That could make it a very big book. Janice is having a little trouble, but I think we can help her through it.

Fri. Sept. 22, 1972

John and Barbara got back Wednesday afternoon. Even though John had a bad tooth ache, there was no doubting the excitement they felt about the Montana property – it looks real good. Last night, they asked me how I felt about it, and I told them it sounded great. The only reservation I have is about going there alone. I really want to take a woman with me. It's lonely enough here, it would be unbearable up there. I remember what it was like at Trancas when Pamela was working. Wednesday night was dull, except for one incident; Martin and Karen and Tom K. came up, and Martin and Tom started a game to get Karen and Dee into swinging. It started as a group massage with the idea that everyone is going to get turned on and they'd switch. What happened was Karen got turned off early in the game and they left. Then Tom found another couple who weren't turned off, and they started. Dee freaked! She came upstairs and fell apart on me. Tom came up to talk to her, but she wanted nothing to do with him. They're going to have to make some heavy decisions pretty soon; he's either got to change or he'll lose her. I don't think he deserves her, but she's got some changes to go through also. Jim found out Kris is on the outs with her parents, and living with a girlfriend. I just don't know what her story is.

Thurs. Sept. 28, 1972

I haven't written in a while, and it's not because I've been busy. Actually, I've been doing very little. Marty asked how I'd feel about selling memberships while the Ranch is in escrow. I admitted I'm having trouble just writing the newsletter. What a paradoxical place I'm in! I want John and Barbara to get the

179

Montana deal, but I don't want it at the expense of Sandstone. Not now. Not after three years of personal turmoil that seems to be on the verge of paying off. Marty and Sue told me they aren't going. Sue added, "That is, if we're even invited." It doesn't take a very perceptive person to know they aren't going to be invited. The vibes are really terrible when they're all in the same room. I'm kind of caught in the middle; John and Barbara and I have a good rapport, but I think it's partly based on the belief, true or false, that I'm going with them. Would it change if I told them I have doubts? Also, Marty and Sue relate well to me most of the time, so I'm in their confidence as well. When all this shit hits the big fan, there are going to be some heavy trips come down, and that's going to happen when the sale is final. Who is really going? What are the rest going to do? Do we get anything out of this, or is it just sent down the hill with, "Bye, bye. It's been a trip." A lot of my questions and indecision center on the movie. Like Marty said, "When it comes out, individually and collectively we're going to get a lot of offers." Why shouldn't we capitalize on that notoriety? It's a hell of an opportunity. The other question is – are we going to make any money out of it? Jonathan said he talked to John about it, and we are. Of course, that was before the Montana thing broke. Does it depend on whether we go to Montana or not? This has to be brought up. None of us are listed on any legal document that I'm aware of, so we have no legal recourse. Pretty dumb of us! Camille came up today and it was beautiful! Finally, I had someone I could share things with. I told her almost everything, including the fact that I'm 39 years old and in a position of attaining some notoriety. Like Jonathan said, "Anyone who sees the film will have no reason to doubt your integrity, Tom. You come across so honest and open – and compassionate." According to him, I'm practically the star. I'm not sure what that'll do to my ego! Kathy called Sunday to tell me she won $15, 400.00 on the quiz show, but she changed her mind about giving me the money, even though she admitted she didn't need it. Okay, so what. I wasn't counting on it anyway. I asked her if she'd like to go to Kirk's wedding next week. She's coming up tomorrow night to tell me – she has to talk to John, in Chicago, first. What bullshit! I may tell her to just forget it. I woke up on a real bummer this morning, thanks to last night. I've about given up on Dee, she may be too fused with Tom to break it. Then Bunny laid a whole trip on me about Jonathan, Dr. Tom. She's getting no sex, and can't understand why he's chasing "cute little girls." I tried to explain the difference, and that I saw a built-in rejection in Jon's selection process. I told her it probably had to do with his fears about the movie

180

and ego-reinforcement. I considered making love with her, but got no vibes from her. Marcelle was up last Saturday, but so was Pamela. I felt completely inhibited. Still no word from Kristine. Marcelle asked me if I'd break a rule and take her to my cottage. Of course I will! My hand (from writing), my head and my gut are all tired.

Friday, Sept. 29, 1972

I don't really feel like writing tonight, but there are some things I'd better record. So...Sandstone is sold. I don't think the full impact has hit yet, but I'm feeling so many different emotions it's hard to sort them out. Some resentments, some relief; it's finally happened. Now is the time to make decisions, no more fantasy, what goes down now is real, irrevocable. John and Barbara are going back to Montana next week, and asked me to go along. We'd stop off in Oregon for Kirk's wedding, then go to Montana. I told them no, I didn't want to be restricted or restrict. I'm really not looking forward to the next few weeks here. A lot is going to happen, and it's mostly pure emotion. How can I reject John and Barbara? That's a heavy one. It's going to be hard for all of us to handle. I love them so much, and I feel that their rejection of me will be so total. You're either with them or against them. I feel I have to stray and make it on my own, I've depended on them long enough.

Mon. Oct. 2, 1972

All that's recorded here has happened in two short months – August and September. To write a book about this place would take a chapter for each week! Kathy came up Friday afternoon and left after supper. She's still playing the same game, laying trips on me right and left, scared I might have fun with someone else. She came back Saturday and spent the night. Sunday, I explained her game to her, like the difference between, "Can I stay in the cottage tonight?" and "I really want to stay in the cottage tonight, but of course that's up to you." It's the difference between honesty and game playing. Strange vibes after dinner. Jon and Bunny and Marty and Sue know I'm not going to Montana. Barbara got mad at me twice tonight; once about the pie and once about the TV. Really jumped on my head. Janice didn't take Michael with her, and I'm very glad. Kathy is taking me to Oregon this week and Barbara says I get no money, that's where she's coming from. Oh, and she jumped on me about the typesetting, also.

181

Tues. Oct. 3, 1972

Went downtown with Doug today, and told him I wasn't going to Montana and why. He was surprised and a little upset. "Wow. A community of three." That's how it looks right now. When we got back, I confronted Marty about his attitude regarding the club, and future activities we might do together. He wants to get further away from membership, more into management, whereas I want the opposite. I still see success coming from a more integral relationship. We have interesting differences. His mood and attitude toward me changed abruptly – I'm no longer an ally against John and Barbara. Funny thing is, Sue kept siding with me. This could change their thinking. Marty may think twice about not going to Montana. Had a nice long talk with Jonathan tonight about the movie. He wants me to look at some scenes with me and Nanci; got most of it cut now, and wants my opinion. That's not going to be easy, but I think I can handle it now. He warned me that it was very real. Still no word from Kris. Nanci has been gone two months, and if she walked in today and wanted to come back, I'd take her. Marty says I have a "father" thing, and there may be some truth to that. Then I think of Eleanor P. and I think I see things in a pretty good perspective. Actually, I think he envies some of the "little girls" I'm with, but they don't buy his trip. Besides, they're not that little. I'm looking forward to my first P.R. trip tomorrow to L.B. State College (Hartman & Fithian). I'm glad Kathy isn't going, she likes to bust my pontificating. Like Saturday night with Myrna. She's one more on my short list.

Wed. Oct. 11, 1972

The trip to Oregon is over and I'm back – and glad of it. It was a very trying six days. I tried to get Kathy off her fantasy trip, we even had a big scene this morning before she finally left. This is going to take a while – there's so much; the history I learned from Mag and Ron, the feeling about my family, Our experiences with Dave and Connie, and the couple in Sacramento, Bud and Gay. Kathy and I left last Wednesday around midnight. I was caressing her while driving, and she liked it so much she opened her pants. She finally had an orgasm, then later admitted she faked it. That was just the beginning. I finally just turned off to her, and that really freaked her. She got into all kinds of manipulations to get to me, including some guilt trips. Kirk's wedding was a complete farce. I didn't see love, affection, or feelings of any kind. I had a long talk with him Friday morning that revealed a lot. He's trying to live up to a lot of

182

peoples' expectations. I had very little opportunity to talk to his sister, Kristen, or Linda, the bride, but it wouldn't have done much good. Kristen is pretty much the same place as Brandi. Linda has no idea where she is. As long as she has some identity as someone's daughter or Kirk's wife, she'll be happy. The rest of the family is the same place they've always been, so I can't relate to them. Dad, at least, accepts what I'm doing and who I am. I enjoyed meeting and talking to Bub and Gay Sunday afternoon. They're every interested in our thing, at least from an intellectual standpoint. It threatens Gay, but not enough to keep her from experimenting. Spent Sunday night with Ron and Mag. She was interested in how Marty is doing, and gave me some background on Jonathan and Bunny. I think it's important to log all those experiences, because it will affect how I relate to others. I felt uncomfortable enough with Ron and Mag that I turned down their offer to spend the night. We drove down to Monterey and got a motel room. Spent Monday and Monday night with Dave and Connie, then left early and drove to Big Sur. I had a nice talk with a couple at the Big Sur Inn – I hope they come visit us. She was very nice, but Kathy didn't like them. But it was about that time Kathy started thinking badly about everything – especially if I liked it. I guess when Bunny said, "Tom did everything right this time with Kris, and still got screwed," she should've pointed out the one mistake I made – I picked the wrong girl. But that's been my problem all along. If it wasn't, I would be with one right now. And be much happier.

Thur. Oct. 12, 1972
History of the movie.
Ron Wilton was in New York working on distribution of "Darkness, Darkness" with Kent Carroll of Grove Press. Jonathan Dana joined Arrikas just before completion of the film. Kent asked Ron if they'd be interested in doing a film on Sandstone. Ron had never heard of it, so they wrote requesting literature, then discussed it. They came here July 4th weekend of '71 to look it over. Mag was already considering leaving at that time. If anything, Ron simply acted as a catalyst. Anyway, Ron and Mag were written out of any interest in the movie. Then, after Barney Rosset couldn't, or wouldn't, put any money in the film, Grove Press was dropped as distributor. So the two individuals who started the whole thing got nothing out of it. Jonathan moved in here in Jan. of '72, and was showing "Darkness, Darkness. I got the impression that he and Bunny had worked on it. Actually, they had practically nothing to do with it. David Espar

183

was Arrikas's director, but he too was eventually dropped from the film. So John and Barbara and Jonathan and Bunny formed Filedae Films. Some might say Grove press and Arrikas got sold out. I know it was a heavy load on Jonathan's head to write them both off, and John and Barbara got the whole thing their way. I remember Barbara telling me back in March that they were thinking of dropping the whole project. "Too much bad karma attached to it." They had gone beyond the contractual agreement regarding time to start production. Also, Jon and Bunny were having some very loud fights with each other. John had to finally tell them to take their fights outside or move out. I remember getting a little nervous when I saw them reading books on documentary film production. They expressed the opinion to me that Barbara is basically very weak, and they wonder how long John is going to put up with her hanging on to him for support and security. It's going to be interesting to see what Bunny thinks tomorrow when they get back. John and Barbara don't have anything to sweat. They've got the Toad and they'll have the money.

Thurs. Oct. 12, 1972
Mag said she'd been miserable for about three months before she left in late Oct. '71. I want to contact John H. about sale back in '69 that fell through.

Sunday, Oct. 15, 1972
Very difficult weekend. They got back Friday evening, and it was really a hassle after supper. I didn't see anything, but Barbara was so mad she almost smacked Sue. After Marty and Sue left, John and Barbara and I had a talk. John was offering his prognostication for the future. Marty has to try and do his thing to compete with John. Sue will leave him. John gives him a 1% chance of succeeding. The failure will be his downfall. He said that I'd surprised him; he'd expected me to fall for Kathy's trip. That really bothered me. I told him I still had some changes to make, but I'd come that far. They expect me to go with them. I'm going to tell them tomorrow night. Gay Talese came up Saturday night, and brought a girl named Linda. She's a stewardess (Flight Attendant) and I really enjoyed her. Unfortunately, I didn't have a chance to relate to her; just too much interference from other people and responsibilities. We did go for a walk, and I could talk to her. I told her I'd like to get to know her better, and she said, "You mean you want to make love with me?" I replied, "Yes, that too." But there was more involved than just that. Gay had a long meeting with John and Barbara that

184

wasn't too successful. He's coming up to the meeting tomorrow night. Marty said, "He's fair game." I see the same manipulations coming, or in progress, as went down over the movie. There's no way I can put all my feelings into words. I have nothing against John and Barbara for wanting to go to Montana, but the mechanisms are causing a lot of bad karma. I hope this doesn't develop into a power struggle between Marty and me. I'm not sure what is happening, but it feels like the same thing that happened when Albert and Carlos tried to buy it. Instead, Carlos bought the Rams.

Wed. Oct. 18, 1972

So Monday night I announced my decision to not go to Montana. Barbara thought it was a wise decision, John said nothing. I kept putting off telling them, but Gay started on this long harangue about the book he wanted to do. This after John and Barbara told him they wouldn't cooperate with him on a personal basis, which means they'll talk about Sandstone, but not themselves. He ran down the whole thing on the Esquire article, which he did write. John and Barbara's reaction was less negative than I expected, but there was a definite cooling. We still haven't discussed the future, but I think we will when "Hot & Cool Sex" is at the printer. It could be the catalyst that gets Nexus Publications off the ground. We're looking at a net profit of around five grand. Who is going to get how much of that? We'll have to formally set up Nexus to sell the book, can't very well have double-signature checks with the upcoming physical distance involved. My love life is nil. Kathy is coming up this evening – which doesn't excite me much. Gay is turned on to her though, so that might be fun to watch – literally.

Sunday, Oct. 22, 1972

I remember the Monday night Sondra left, and what she said to me. "Tom, you've got to get out of here. Please get out! Don't you know what this place is? This is a scientific experiment. They're testing us to see how much pain the human mind can stand." That was shortly after the night I did my big Freak Out. The Saturday night Pamela went downstairs with Ron, and I ended up quivering and crying on Sondra's bed. I cried when she left, too. But so did everybody else – I'm having trouble tonight. Then there was Camille, and Nanci, and Kris. I remember telling Mag what Sondra had said, and instead of laughing, she said, "Wow! That's very heavy." A strange reaction. So I'm asking myself why? Now,

185

I can't freak out, at least not in public. Too many people look at me as being "The Strong One." Ha! If they only knew how my jaws ache from clenching my teeth. Like tonight. One nice thing about Sunday (about the only thing) is that nobody can dump their shit on my head for a few days. Except maybe Bunny – again. I know they say I ask for it, and maybe I do, but somebody better. Otherwise, there'd be a lot more violence up here. When I left Trancas and broke up with Pamela, one reason was that I was tired of her, the kids, and our personal friends using me as their personal toilet. Everyone had questions and needed help. Finally, I had to find an environment and people that I could ask questions of. I didn't know what the questions were, but I knew I couldn't ask them in that environment. So I came to Sandstone. Well, I've got a hell of a lot of answers now, but I still don't know all the questions. It doesn't matter any more. So I've suffered. The period of two weeks when I couldn't stop my teeth chattering, and my muscles were cramping all night. More psychological pain than I knew existed. For what? So I can answer bigger, harder questions? That's not enough.

Tues. Oct. 24, 1972

Since I'm having trouble deciding what to do about Gay, I think I'd better write about it. If he's living here, he's going to have an effect on everything. Like the trip with Kathy. All I was trying to tell him Saturday morning was that I could see no reason why my relationship with her, or hers with me, should be a necessary part of their conversation. The only reason I could see for him to tell Kathy how I felt about her was to get her to switch beds. If he really understood the concept of honest communication, he'd realize that Kathy already knew how I felt about her. For her to come to me and claim to be so upset by what he'd told her indicated that they were both playing games, or she really didn't trust me anymore. I think all three could be true. I've gotten feedback from a lot of the family, and it's all the same; I was really turned on by Linda until I started questioning her motives. It's not too difficult to see that Gay doesn't like (hates) women. So either she's a star fucker, she doesn't know where he's at, or she wants the subtle form of punishment he gives. Coupled with her work with Suicide Prevention, I'd bet on the last one. I think she wants to be used. It's too bad, but then I have to remember she's where most people are. I do wish Gay's wife could come out for a weekend. It would really facilitate things. I believe he wants to change, but first he has to be in a position to do that. I don't see him

186

doing that as long as he's here without a strong commitment. Only that will expose him to himself. I still feel he can write about us, but it would be better if he understood us.

Friday, Oct. 27, 1972

John said the other night that I have trouble with "dead horses." Their behavior towards me the last couple of days would seem to indicate I'm considered a dead horse. If John continues his bad sarcasm, I'll have to say something. I asked Marty why he told Leslie and her boyfriend the place would be closed in December. At first, he tried to deny it, then changed saying he was sure they wouldn't join anyway. I'm really separated from everybody lately. There's just nobody here, in or out of the family, that I want to relate to. I've been on the ragged edge a few times, and I guess it'll get worse. The closing of Sandstone isn't going to be "out like a lamb" for sure.

Sunday, Nov. 26, 1972

It's been a long time, a lot has happened that I should have recorded and didn't. Nexus Publications is a reality as of two weeks ago when John, Barbara and I signed the papers and opened the bank account. My personal life has been less than exciting, although Dale and Carol from Indiana are the most interesting people I've met since Janet R. They are really beautiful! I only wish we could have gotten as close as all three of us wanted to. I gather Ralph Yaney and Marty will be using the Sandstone name in their new venture – a therapy restaurant. Never make it. The "family" vibes are zero. I almost smacked Marty Saturday evening. I've decided that Janice won't be with me in future, she just isn't in touch with the philosophy, she just wants to be taken care of. I love her, but I need people with me who understand the philosophy and want to try and live it. I don't think John and Barbara are taking me seriously about starting another club, but I am. Although I'm not sure why. Why do I want to continue seeing frightened people not doing what they feel? Actually denying their feelings consciously. I've had some interesting experiences with women, but almost all of them are afraid. The experience with Barbara, Jim Borden's girlfriend, is a perfect example. It happened last Friday. She came up after supper. I took it very slowly, I didn't want to scare her, and everything went well. We ended up in the cottage. Everything progressed nicely until she suddenly said, "Oh, no!" Then there was Jerry's date, Ann, and Paul Paige's Terri. All scared. And let's not

187

forget Gay's Linda. We're in the pool, and suddenly she says, "Stay away, Tom. Please."

Wed. Jan. 10, 1973

Let's go back. The club officially closed December 28th. The last party was the night before. Mom and dad brought my boys, Rusty and Glenn, up on the 23rd. Patty moved in with me on the 16th. It was the night before that she and Danny and I had our talk at their apartment. What it came down to was me saying, "I'll have a Primary or Satellite Relationship with her or drop out completely." She replied, "I'll have any relationship I can with Tom." Danny said nothing. The next day, she called and asked if she could come up and talk. When she arrived, she told me that her decision was to have a Primary with me. Roughly, that's how it started, and we've been together 25 days so far. So much has happened, it seems like much longer, but I feel that all of our experiences have really deepened our love for each other. There are seven us still living here; John and Barbara, Jonathan and Bunny, Doug, and us. Interestingly, the Foundation is still supporting the other five. Patty and I are renting our small house trailer from Tom D., and buying our own food. The only things we're not paying for are water and electricity. Things were so bad around the first of the year, we loaned John and Barbara $500.00. We finally got the first copies of "Hot & Cool Sex" on Jan. 2nd. We picked them up just before the radio show we appeared on, so I didn't get a chance to look at them until this morning. John helped himself to some copies out of our car before we got up. So the first thing we heard was what a lousy job they'd done on the books. The biggest problem was that they were cut crooked. What nobody knew was that he picked some that had slipped past the binder. His man was trying to trim them in big stacks. As soon as the binder caught him, he made him stop, but a few had slipped through. The other major complaint was that the type didn't line up on facing pages. I don't think we've gotten a positive vibe from them since. Maybe a few from John, but none from Barbara; she has a big resentment against me and Patty. I know that some of it is because I didn't take her advice and have Kathy move in with me – damn the feelings, she's got money! That's all Barbara can see. She was even nice to me until she decided the book wasn't going to make it. Now, we hardly speak to each other. She makes juvenile remarks around us, and accuses me of failing, which is exactly what I don't need right now. I'm sure she's expressed her opinion to the others, and that affects their behavior toward us. I

188

know of phone calls I've received when Doug didn't give me the message. I tried to talk to John about the phone, but every suggestion is met with, "That costs money." We're at the point where we have to sit by the phone. Brandi came up and the three of us enjoyed a very nice evening together, got stoned, ate lots of munchies and I sat on the floor watching Brandi and Patty on the couch in black light. I hear they've changed the beginning of the movie – again. Talked to Marty the other day, and he told me it looked like he'd either have to get John to give him the name, Sandstone, buy it, or go to court. I told him to get a cheap lawyer. He said he's still an officer of the Foundation, and they're still using the Institute letterhead. They're in the same category as Albert, Dave and Oralia, and others; don't mention them to John and Barbara. The damned Escrow still hasn't closed which is probably the reason for all the bad vibes. Barbara hates being that close to money and not be able to touch it. Jonathan and Bunny talked to them about doing some additional taping for the movie, but they said they couldn't right now, they were too anxious about the sale. Barbara said, "Let's face it, if we can't sell this place, everything is off including the movie." I wonder if that includes Nexus? When we walked in the North house today, John was coming out of the kitchen with a banana. He held out the peel to me and said, "Here, Tom, why don't you take this outside and slip on it."

Just a joke? Maybe, but it's black humor right now and he knows it.

Epilogue

I remember sitting in the living room of the North house one night with John and Barbara. They were back in town after one of their trips to settle the property sale once and for all. It seems the new buyers weren't quite as financially solvent as John and Barbara had been led to believe, and they were now considering the distinct possibility o being forced to foreclose on them. We were talking about that, and other sales they hadn't been able to finalize, when Barbara told me she was beginning to honestly feel that the property, Sandstone Ranch, wasn't going to let go of them until 'it' was sure the new owners would put it to the same type of use. That may seem strange to some people, but if you ever lived on that property, you'd know just how Magical it was, and not even blink an eye at her statement.

Now Barbara's prophecy seems to be coming true to some extent. After almost a year of hassling, the place has been taken over by someone who plans to open another club similar to Sandstone Retreat. Obviously, there is no way anyone will be able to reopen "Sandstone." What happened there in the five years of operation were so unique, and involved very special people, that it can never be replicate. But it will be interesting to watch the whole thing – from a distance.

Patty and I are finally out of the house trailer and are away from it – at least physically. We spent our first nine months together in that house trailer, and if you want to find out if a relationship will really work, try living in a 27-foot trailer! We made it, an now we're "doing our own thing." No plans for starting another Retreat, but possibly starting a small community based on the same philosophy. We definitely plan on finding a less energy-draining method of supporting ourselves than operating a Retreat.

We hear that Jonathan and Bunny have finished editing the movie, and are showing it to prospective distributors. They say it's really something to see on a full-size screen. I must admit I have mixed feelings about that part o my involvement in Sandstone. When we participated in that project, it was supposedly going to benefit Sandstone. That was a major motivating factor in the decision many of us made to take part in it, and make it the best portrayal of the lifestyle possible. Now, of course, all of that has changed. None of the family, except John and Barbara and Jonathan and Bunny will materially benefit from it. And there are some, both within the family and the membership, who would prefer it never be shone. Some of the members risked a great deal by agreeing to appear in the movie. I only hope their trust and conviction weren't misplaced.

All of us who spent that last eventful year together are pretty spread out now. Patty and I bought some land in a beautiful rural area out of California. John and Barbara have settled even farther away. Jon and Bunny are still in Malibu working on getting the movie released. Marty and Sue might be involved in the new club opening at the Ranch. The rest, Janice and her beautiful daughter Sherri, Doug, and the others who spent some portion o their lives living with us are spread out all over the country. We have very little communication with any of them. I do know that others, besides Patty and me, are still interested in the community lifestyle, and may be looking for ways to implement that interest.

Once you've been part of a community, it's difficult to go back to that 'other' value system.

It's comforting and easy to look back on that whole experience with the dubious benefit of hindsight, and attempt to analyze it. But, as we used to tell so many others, there is no one answer or explanation or Sandstone. It was a completely subjective experience for each individual who visited or lived there. No one will ever able to write about it from the outside, because to do that he or she would have to get outside themselves. I can look back on it, and know what value it had for me.

One of the most important things I did learn in those long five years was a new value system. A lot of traditional values I lived with before I joined the organization got totally destroyed and replaced with other more lie-enhancing ones. But like any other philosophy, it shouldn't be accepted by any individual in its totality. What Patty and I are in the process of doing now is re-examining the whole philosophy, and adjusting it to our lifestyle instead of trying to adjust ourselves to the whole philosophy. I do believe that was one of the biggest

191

problems many of us had at Sandstone. The philosophy stressed the ultimate value of being an individual, and as such, each of us has to decide what our own personal lifestyle will be.

If other places similar to Sandstone do open up, it will be interesting to see how closely they will try to duplicate our environment. I hope they don't try too hard. Sandstone did wonderful things for me and others who were there. Hopefully, the new experiments will be able to build on our experience, and have even more to offer you, the reader.